ANTON CHEKHOV

The Cherry Orchard

ANTON CHEKHOV

The Cherry Orchard

Translated, with an Introduction and Notes, by

Sharon Marie Carnicke

Hackett Publishing Company, Inc.
Indianapolis/Cambridge

Copyright © 2010 by Hackett Publishing Company, Inc.

14 13 12 11 10   1 2 3 4 5 6 7

For further information, please address
   Hackett Publishing Company, Inc.
   P.O. Box 44937
   Indianapolis, Indiana 46244-0937

   www.hackettpublishing.com

Cover design by Brian Rak and Elizabeth L. Wilson
Text design by Elizabeth L. Wilson
Composition by William Hartman
Printed at Sheridan Books, Inc.

Library of Congress Cataloging-in-Publication Data
Chekhov, Anton Pavlovich, 1860–1904.
    [Vishnevyi sad. English]
    The cherry orchard / Anton Chekhov; translated, with
an introduction and notes, by Sharon Marie Carnicke.
        p. cm.
    Includes bibliographical references.
    ISBN 978-1-60384-310-2 — ISBN 978-1-60384-309-6 (pbk.)
    I. Carnicke, Sharon Marie, 1949- II. Title.
    PG3456.V5C37 2010
    891.72'3—dc22
                                        2010016299

Contents

Acknowledgments

I would like to thank Gene Nye of Lion Theatre Company (New York) for giving me the opportunity to translate Chekhov's *Three Sisters*. I learned a tremendous amount about Chekhov, translating, and acting from his rehearsals with the company. This experience proved invaluable when the talented Russian émigré director, Lev Vainstein, then requested a translation by me of *The Cherry Orchard*, which he directed first for New York University's graduate program in acting and later for other venues.

In fact, I owe much to all the directors who have staged my translations and the actors in their productions. The directors include John David Lutz (University of Evansville), whose beautiful production of *The Seagull* won for me a translation award from the American College Theatre Festival at the Kennedy Center (Washington, D.C.), and the late John Blankenchip (University of Southern California), who continually supported my work. The actors include Louisa Abernathy (of A/ACT in Los Angeles) and Setrak Bronzian, who taught me the power of physical humor. Because I try to convey in English what I hear in my mind as I read the Russian, I am particularly honored by the émigré directors who have chosen my translations. In addition to Lev Vainstein, I also thank Albert Makhtsier (Theatre in Action in New York) and Eugene Lazerev (formerly of the Moscow Art Theatre).

I also want to thank five close colleagues and friends. The émigré movement teacher Edward Rozinsky (Miami, Florida) generously checked my information on pronunciation and the meanings implicit in the characters' names. Mary Joan Negro (Classics Alive and the University of Southern California), R. Andrew White (Valparaiso University), and Leslie Wagner (New York City) offered valuable feedback as I finalized this volume. My friend Patricia Padilla (Los Angeles, California) knew nothing of my contract with Hackett, yet she serendipitously gave me a gift that made work on this publication easier than I could have imagined; she gave me a complete set of Anton Chekhov's works in Russian.

Brian Rak and James Hullett of Hackett Publishing Company invited me to create this volume. Despite numerous productions of my translations, their appearance in print is due to the efforts of these two creative men, and I am grateful to them.

Finally, I thank a number of my students at the University of Southern California: Rose Leisner, who helped me proof, edit, type, and scan this volume, and the members of my freshman seminars (Checking Out Chekhov, fall 2008 and fall 2009), who influenced my introduction to this edition.

Notes on the Translation

Source and Transliterations

The text of *The Cherry Orchard* and quotations from Chekhov's other plays and letters are taken from A. P. Chekhov, *Polnoe sobranie sochinenii i pisem v tridtsati tomakh* [*The Complete Works and Letters in Thirty Volumes*], Moscow: Nauka, 1974–1984. This edition reprints Chekhov's 1902 revisions, made in connection with the first publication of his complete works by A. F. Marx.

Rather than using a scholarly system for transliterating the Russian alphabet into English, I use more informal conventions that assist readers with the pronunciations of names and words (for example, "Stanislavsky" instead of "Stanislavskii," "Sergeyevich" for "Sergeevich," and "Maria" rather than "Mar'ia").

In my translations, I retain all ellipses used by Chekhov as they appear in the Russian texts. Whenever I elide material from a quotation in my introduction and notes, I use an ellipsis in brackets to mark the place where an abridgement has been made.

Money and Measures

In the Russian monetary system, there are one hundred kopecks in each ruble. I retain these terms, but I recalculate other unfamiliar Russian measures (such as "versts," "desiatins," and "poods") into English equivalents (miles, acres, and pounds).

Russian Names

All names are given as they appear in the Russian texts because they offer valuable emotional information. Actors who understand Russian names can use them effectively in performance.

Formal address in Russian consists of the first name and patronymic, for example, "Anton Pavlovich" (Anton Son-of-Pavel) or "Maria Pavlovna" (Maria Daughter-of-Pavel). When used together, the name and patronymic serve as "Mr.," "Miss," and "Mrs.," signifying the speaker's respect. For example, in *The Cherry Orchard,* when the servants call Lopakhin "Yermolay Alekseyevich" (Yermolay Son-of-Aleksey), they show him respect as a rich man. Notice that the landowner Ranyevskaya is also called "Lyubov Andreyevna" by most of the characters in the play, thus betokening the respect due to a woman of her age and class.

Rarely do Russians use surnames; these serve primarily to identify a family connection (as in the cast lists), to refer to famous personages (such as authors or actors), or to introduce complete strangers. Sometimes using a last name alone is a sign of disrespect, an insult. While perhaps not consciously insulting, most of the characters in *The Cherry Orchard* call Yepikhodov by his last name, suggesting their somewhat superior attitude toward him.

First names are used only by one's intimate friends and family, but can always be used by anyone when speaking to children and servants. Russian is also particularly rich in nicknames (called "pet names" among Russian speakers). These are formed by adding diminutive endings to the first name. These diminutives can be piled onto the name almost endlessly and signify warmth, emotional closeness, and sympathy between people. A first-degree diminutive is common in the family circle. For example, Gayev calls his sister by the diminutive "Lyuba," for "Lyubov." Most of the servants are called by their pet names: for example, "Dunyasha" for "Avdotya" and "Yasha" (whose formal first name is not even given in the cast list). Notably, Lyubov Andreyevna's adopted daughter is usually called "Varya" instead of the more formal "Vavara," a form of address that tends to equate her with the servants. Also notable is the fact that the oldest servant in the household, Firs, is called only by his formal first name, never a pet name. Perhaps this form betokens the fact that, by virtue of his age, he deserves a bit more respect than the younger servants.

In brackets in the cast list, I give specific information on the characters' names.

Pronunciation

Unlike English, which uses primary and secondary stresses, Russian stresses only one syllable in each name or word. All other syllables are given equal and minimal weight. To assist with pronunciation, whenever a Russian name or word appears in the text for the first time, I have marked the stressed syllable with an accent.

Russian vowels tend to be softer than English vowels. *A* is always "ah," as in "father" ("Áhn-yah" for Anya; "Yáh-shah" for Yasha). *E* sounds like "eh," as in "pet" ("Gáh-yehv" for Gayev). *I* is always "ee," as in "feel" ("Péesh-cheek" for Pishchik). *O* resembles "aw," as in "dog," never "oh" ("Traw-fée-mov" for Trofimov; "Seh-myáwn" for Semyon; "Yeh-pee-kháw-dawv" for "Yepikhodov"). *U* is "oo," as in "fool" ("Doon-yáh-sha" for Dunyasha).

Introduction

A Taste for Chekhov's Drama

When studying Russian literature for the first time in college, I found to my surprise that Chekhov's famous plays left me cold. I had expected to be swept away because my acting teachers equated Chekhov with Shakespeare whenever they spoke of great classic drama, and I had grown up with a passion for Shakespeare. My Russian professor told me that Chekhov, like olives, is an acquired taste. Every time I now re-read one of his elegantly simple and yet richly complex plays, I find something new to delight me. By means of this Introduction, I offer you a brief guide to the Chekhov I have come to know and love.

In *The Cherry Orchard*, Chekhov brings his unique angle of vision to a set of memorable characters. He tells each of their stories with such insight into human experience that he provokes laughter, then tears, and sometimes both at the same time. After viewing Michael Cacoyannis' 2002 filmed version of *The Cherry Orchard*, one reviewer wrote: "We are left as always with Chekhov's effortless humanity, the sheer psychological acuity he brought to the loves, hopes and inchoate longings of his characters."[1] In this, Chekhov's last play, he also perfects the counterintuitive techniques in playwriting that he had developed in his earlier plays. These innovations make *The Cherry Orchard* seem at once an "antitheatrical play" and a "theatrical revolution"; as one of Chekhov's biographers put it, his last play is his "ultimate theatrical coup d'état."[2] In short, *The Cherry Orchard* can be read as a quintessential example of the Chekhovian play.

But what kind of a play did Chekhov write? This question is not so very easy to answer. Since the premiere of *The Cherry Orchard* in 1904, spectators and scholars alike have debated its genre, its artistic style, and even the content of its story.

1. Kenneth Turan, "The Cherry Orchard," *Los Angeles Times: Calendar Live,* April 5, 2002, http://www.calendarlive.com/movies/reviews, accessed April 29, 2009.

2. Donald Rayfield, *The Cherry Orchard: Catastrophe and Comedy* (New York: Twayne Publishers, 1994), 8.

In terms of genre, has Chekhov written a comedy or a tragedy? He certainly seemed to think it comic. When he delivered the play to the Moscow Art Theatre for its premiere staging, he called it "not a drama at all, but a comedy, in places a farce."[3] In 1933, a British reviewer agreed, calling Chekhov "a thoroughly amusing and flippant dramatist."[4] But the play's first director, Konstantin Stanislavsky, thought otherwise. After reading it for the first time, "I cried like a woman," he told the author. "For the ordinary person, this is a tragedy."[5] In 1923, American audiences tended to agree with Stanislavsky, seeing in this play, as in all of Chekhov's plays, the author's "Slavic temperament [which] feeds upon self-deprecation, upon pessimism."[6]

Regarding style, has Chekhov created "the supreme achievement of the naturalistic movement in modern theatre," as J. L. Styan would have it,[7] or does *The Cherry Orchard* "imperceptibly cross over into symbolism," as the great Russian poet Andrey Bely argued?[8] Productions have had it both ways. In 1904 Stanislavsky created a detailed illusion of the reality of life on a Russian estate. In fact, Stanislavsky used his own estate, Lyubimovka, as his model for the production's sets. After all, he knew that Chekhov had been writing the play while on a visit there with his wife, Olga Knipper (a leading actress of the Moscow Art Theatre). Knipper wrote to Chekhov during rehearsals to tell him that she found herself sitting on a "sofa that is placed [on the stage] just where it was at

3. Chekhov to M. P. Lilina, September 15, 1903, in A. P. Chekhov *Polnoe sobranie sochinenii i pisem: Pis'ma* [Complete Works and Letters: Letters], vol. 11 (Moscow: Nauka, 1982), 248. This multi-volume edition is hereafter cited as *Pis'ma* [Letters].

4. Leslie Rees, review of *The Cherry Orchard, Era,* October 11, 1933, in Victor Emeljanow, ed., *Chekhov: The Critical Heritage* (Boston: Routledge and Kegan Paul, 1981), 380.

5. K. S. Stanislavsky to A. P. Chekhov, October 22, 1903, in K. S. Stanislavsky, *Sobranie sochinenii* [Collected Works], vol. 7 (Moscow: Iskusstvo, 1995), 506.

6. John Corbin, review of *Three Sisters, New York Times,* January 31, 1923, in Emeljanow, ed., *Chekhov: The Critical Heritage,* 241.

7. J. L. Styan, *Chekhov in Performance: A Commentary on the Major Plays* (New York: Cambridge University Press, 1971), 239.

8. Andrey Bely, "The Cherry Orchard," in Laurence Senelick, trans. and ed., *Russian Dramatic Theory from Pushkin to the Symbolists* (Austin: University of Texas Press, 1981), 90.

Lyubimovka, in the connecting room, just by our dining room."[9]
In contrast, the 1977 New York Shakespeare Festival production,
directed by Andrei Serban, stressed the play's nonrealism. The
actors moved through an expanse of empty space, surrounded only
by random pieces of furniture and some long-abandoned toys, set
against a background of starkly beautiful cherry trees.[10]

Some critics have also argued that Chekhov's comic emphasis on
the inability of characters to communicate with each other marks
his play as an early example of twentieth-century absurdism. A
1990 production in Moscow, directed by Leonid Trushkin, brought
this view to life. Prompted by Gayev's Act I speech in praise of a
century-old cupboard, Trushkin set the play inside an enormous
cupboard with a multitude of doors, each one opening to reveal a
scene unfold; the actors, like marionettes, emerged mechanically
from the cupboard.[11]

And finally, in terms of story, has Chekhov written "a lament
for the dispossessed Russian gentry" or "a call to revolution"?[12]
In the first case, Lyubov Andreyevna and her brother Gayev take
center stage as the orchard's owners; the loss of their ancestral
home anchors the play. When Stanislavsky cast the company's two
strongest actors, himself and Chekhov's wife, as the landowners,
he made the gentry the focus of his production. In the second case,
the political activist Trofimov steps forward and the play registers
as a canny premonition of the 1905 and 1917 Russian revolutions.
Soviet productions from the 1920s through the 1970s tended to
stage the play in this way because this view sympathized with com-
munist propaganda. These productions romanticized Trofimov. He
became a heroic figure who alone speaks the truth among a group
of decadent landowners and a greedy capitalist (in the person of
Lopakhin).[13]

9. Ol'ga Leonardovna Knipper-Chekhova, *Perepiska* [Correspondence], vol. 1
(Moscow: Iskusstvo, 1972), 334.

10. I describe the set as I remember it. For more on this production, see Laurence
Senelick, *The Chekhov Theatre: A Century of the Plays in Performance* (New
York: Cambridge University Press, 1997), 297–99.

11. I describe what I remember. For more, see Senelick, *The Chekhov Theatre*,
354.

12. James N. Loehlin, *Chekhov: The Cherry Orchard* (Cambridge: Cambridge
University Press, 2006), 1.

13. For specific Soviet productions, see Senelick, *The Chekhov Theatre*, 86–88,
and Loehlin, *Chekhov: The Cherry Orchard*, 84–88.

These two options, however, do not exhaust the possibilities. *The Cherry Orchard* could also be about the pangs of unrequited love. Why else would Chekhov spend so much stage time on Lyubov's burning desire for a cad in Paris, Dunyasha's two competing suitors, Varya's painful yearning for Lopakhin, Anya's budding passion for Trofimov, and his for her? Then too, there is the story about how one generation replaces another as the cycle of life moves inexorably forward in time. While Firs (the oldest living person in the play) remembers a time when the orchard was as commercially viable as it is now beautiful, Lopakhin envisions a future in which summer houses and gardens will make the land productive again and bring it a new kind of beauty. In Act IV when Anya (the youngest person in the play) and Trofimov exit into their future lives, her line, "Goodbye, old life!" cedes to his, "Hello, new life!"

Chekhov's letters also suggest other key stories embedded within his play. He sees Charlotta as an important role; and thus he tells the Moscow Art Theatre that "this is the role for Mme. Knipper."[14] He had, in fact, written it for his wife who, like Charlotta, has a German name, was a ventriloquist, and performed card tricks. "Oh, if only you were playing the governess in my play!" he laments to his wife. "That is the best role, I don't like the others."[15] How might we position Charlotta—with her magic tricks, ventriloquism, and lost identity—at the center of Chekhov's play? In regard to the male characters, the author saw Lopakhin as "the central role of the play." Consequently Chekhov attempted to persuade Stanislavsky to play the part, arguing that Lopakhin is "a completely decent person [who] must behave properly, intelligently, not small-mindedly, without tricks up his sleeve."[16] Chekhov also

Portrait of Chekhov, 1902.

14. Chekhov to Vl. I. Nemirovich-Danchenko, November 2, 1903, in *Pis'ma* [Letters], vol. 11, 293.

15. Chekhov to O. L. Knipper, September 29, 1903, in ibid., 259.

16. Chekhov to K. S. Stanislavsky, October 30, 1903, in ibid., 291.

told his wife that, "If [this role] does not go well, then the entire play will miscarry."[17] How might Lopakhin then be seen as the primary protagonist in *The Cherry Orchard*? Acquiring a taste for Chekhov involves setting aside all these debates for a moment and looking at Chekhov on his own terms. Because he broke away from traditional conventions of playwriting to create a new approach to the crafting of plays, I invite you to examine *The Cherry Orchard* first through the lens of Chekhov's innovations in drama and then against the backdrop of his life.

Melodrama Turned Inside Out

Chekhov's meteoritic rise to fame in fiction was precariously balanced against a painfully slow acceptance of his drama. By 1888, at age twenty-eight, Anton Chekhov had already established himself as the greatest living Russian storyteller, second only to the famous novelist Leo Tolstoy (1828–1910), who was then in his sixties. Chekhov had begun to write at age fourteen. While still in high school he submitted short comedic stories under various pseudonyms to popular magazines. His first publication dates from 1879. As a medical student, he churned out hundreds of stories. In 1883 alone he published ninety. When he graduated, he kept writing at the same furious pace. In 1885 he published more than one hundred stories.

At the end of 1885, Chekhov visited his publisher in Russia's cosmopolitan capital of St. Petersburg. He was astonished to learn that people not only read his stories avidly but eagerly awaited his next contributions. His readers, it seemed, were taking him seriously as a writer. "If I had known they were reading me like that," he told his eldest brother, "I would not have written on short order."[18] Three months later, Chekhov received a long, detailed letter that, he said, "surprised me, as if it were a lighting bolt."[19] The nationally famous author Dmitry Grigorovich had written to tell Chekhov that his "real talent," which "far exceeds other writers of the new generation," could translate into a literary career of significance.

17. Chekhov to O. L. Knipper, Ibid., 290.
18. Chekhov to Al. P. Chekhov, January 4, 1886, in A. P. Chekhov *Sobranie sochinenii* [Collected Works], vol. 11 (Moscow: Izdatel'stvo khudozhestvennoi literatury, 1956), 70.
19. Chekhov to D. V. Grigorovich, March 28, 1886, in ibid., 79.

"You are, I am sure, meant to write some exceptional, truly artistic works." But Grigorovich also reprimanded the young writer for obviously hasty and careless writing, telling him to "respect" his own talent or risk "commit[ting] the great moral sin of not fulfilling your calling."[20] Chekhov took heed, began to use his real name for publications, slowed the pace of his writing, and perfected the economical and allusive craft by which he created true masterpieces of short fiction. A scant two years later in October 1888, the Russian Academy of Sciences unanimously voted to give him the prestigious Pushkin Prize for literature. In another two years, Chekhov would himself become a member of that same Academy.

In tandem with fiction, Chekhov had also been writing plays, but fame as a dramatist came much harder and later. He was attracted to the theater from the first. In high school, his father and teachers forbade him from attending the local theater. Such entertainment, after all, could prove a bad influence on a boy. Chekhov still managed to sneak off to see lascivious French farces and operettas, Russian plays by Nikolay Gogol and Alexander Ostrovsky, Shakespeare's classics, and broadly comic vaudevilles. Among the first books that Chekhov bought were translations of Shakespeare's *Hamlet* and *Macbeth*.[21] By the time Chekhov was eighteen, he had written at least two plays (a serious one, *Fatherless,* and a lost vaudeville, *Why the Hen Clucks*).

When he moved to Moscow for medical school, he built his social life around theater: he attended all kinds of performances, befriended actors of the highest rank, and flirted (and more) with actresses. When he decided to marry in 1901, he chose a leading actress of the Moscow Art Theatre, Olga Knipper. Like his early stories, many of his plays were short "jokes," as he called them. Staged widely throughout Russia's provinces, these one-acts provided Chekhov with substantial income, so much that he advised his eldest brother to sit down and write two or three plays. "A play," he said "is a pension fund."[22]

Despite his early infatuation with theater, Chekhov had also begun to criticize the unconvincing melodramatic claptrap and the histrionic acting that was common on nineteenth-century stages.

20. Grigorovich to Chekhov, March 25, 1886, in ibid., 626.

21. Donald Rayfield, *Anton Chekhov: A Life* (New York: Henry Holt, 1997), 59.

22. Chekhov to Al. P. Chekhov, February 21, 1899, in *Pis'ma* [Letters], vol. 3 (Moscow: Nauka, 1976), 164.

He wanted plays and acting to be "just as complex and also just as simple as in life. People eat their dinner, just eat their dinner, yet at the same time their happiness is taking shape and their lives are being smashed."[23] Put another way, "In real life people do not spend every minute shooting each other, hanging themselves, or making declarations of love." Instead, "They eat, drink, flirt, talk nonsense."[24] Chekhov began to experiment with dramatic forms that matched his opinions of theater.

In his longer plays, he turns the usual stories of melodrama inside out by putting action-packed events like duels and fires offstage; nothing much seems to happen onstage. This innovation can best be seen by reading a melodrama, like Dion Boucicault's *The Octoroon* (1859), against *The Cherry Orchard*. Both tell the same basic story: a widow, whose husband left her with nothing but debts, finds that her property will be sold at auction. Boucicault depicts murder, fraud, and a climactic onstage auction. In contrast, Chekhov shows what happens to people between the big incidents in their lives. Every action-packed event in *The Cherry Orchard,* even the auction, happens offstage. Onstage, the characters only wait for and then react to what has happened elsewhere. We watch them spend time, worry, make plans, have coffee, reminisce, tease, converse, flirt, give a party, and cope with bad news that forever changes their lives. After learning of the auction, the widow collapses into a state of shock, while the buyer of her estate expresses his exultant, yet guilty, joy. Nor does Chekhov end the play with these climactic reactions; instead he follows his characters as they pick up their lives, establish new routines, and move on. While Boucicault depicts the external causes that throw lives into turmoil, Chekhov paints the familiar experience of living from day to day. By turning melodrama inside out, he has also effectively redefined the notion of dramatic action as the inner, psychological, often subtle movements of the soul. As one of my students observed, "Chekhov's portrayal of the tedium of life allows the audience to get to the subtleties of the characters and become more personally attached to them."[25]

---

23. Spoken words from 1889, translated by Gordon McVay in *Chekhov's* Three Sisters (London: Bristol Classical Press, 1995), 42.

24. D. Gorodetskii, "Iz vospominanii ob A. P. Chekhove" [Reminiscences of A. P. Chekhov] in *Chekhov i teatr* [Chekhov and the Theater], ed. E. D. Surkov (Moscow: Iskusstvo, 1961), 208–9.

25. Mark Lay, Freshman Seminar: Checking Out Chekhov, University of Southern California, Fall 2008.

Chekhov also refuses to sort his characters into easily identifiable heroes and villains as melodrama does; all his characters are in turn admirable and silly, cruel and kind. While writing *Ivanov* in 1887 (his first full-length play to be staged), Chekhov described his approach:

> Contemporary playwrights fill their plays with angels, villains, and clowns. Go find such types anywhere in Russia! However hard you look, you won't find them anywhere except in plays. [. . .] I wanted to do something original: I didn't bring into it one villain, not one angel (although I couldn't resist the clowns).[26]

Another quick look at Boucicault's *The Octoroon* makes Chekhov's point about angels and villains clear: Boucicault's widow has only one flaw—she lacks business experience. As for the buyer of her land, Mr. McClosky has only one admirable trait, his well-trimmed mustaches. They are heroine and villain personified. In *The Cherry Orchard*, Chekhov's widow may lack business sense, but she understands love very well; in fact, her first name, Lyubov, means "love" in Russian. Her nemesis, Lopakhin, may exceed her in business

Chekhov in Yalta, 1899.

26. Chekhov to Al. P. Chekhov, October 24, 1887, in *Pis'ma* [Letters], vol. 2 (Moscow: Nauka, 1975), 137–38.

savvy, but he is helpless in regard to affairs of the heart. Neither one is fully heroic or fully villainous. With the inclusion of a few clowns, like the clerk, Yepikhodov, who keeps tripping over his own feet, Chekhov creates a dramatic genre that is neither fully comic nor fully tragic. In his plays, nonsense coexists with philosophy and conversations about the weather follow climactic moments that decide characters' fates.

Similar experimentation had rewarded Chekhov lavishly in the realm of fiction, but it was not to be so in drama. In 1889, the selection committee for the Alexandrinsky Theatre in St. Petersburg found his play *The Wood Demon* to be "a beautiful dramatization of a novella, but not a play."[27] Alexander Lensky (Moscow's leading actor) told his good friend Chekhov to "write [only] tales. You refer too scornfully to the stage and to dramatic form. You esteem them too little to write a play."[28]

Flaunting all advice, Chekhov wrote his next play, *The Seagull*, by "mercilessly betraying stage conventions."[29] At its 1897 premiere, the play was audibly booed. Selected as a benefit performance for a famous comic actress of the Alexandrinsky Theatre, *The Seagull* opened to an audience of her fans, who expected broad comedy. The subtlety of Chekhov's new play escaped them. Moreover, critics (who had lobbied against Chekhov's plays) further provoked the crowd's guffaws. Chekhov left the theater midway through the performance, walked the streets in despair, and returned to his home, vowing never to write for the theater again. He told his younger brother, "The play flopped, collapsed with a thud. In the theatre I felt the burdensome tension of perplexity and shame. [. . .] The moral is: it's not worth writing plays."[30] He immediately stopped the play's publication and told his editor, "It wasn't just my play which failed, it was me. [. . .] I will never forget what happened, just as I could never forget, for example, being slapped in the face."[31]

Even so, admiration for Chekhov's plays lurked behind the pervasive abuse. Despite the Alexandrinsky Theatre's rejection of *The*

27. A. P. Chekhov, *Polnoe sobranie sochinenii i pisem: Sochineniia* [The Complete Collected Works and Letters: Works], vol. 11 (Moscow: Izdatel'stvo khudozhestvennoi literatury, 1948), 614.

28. Ibid.

29. Chekhov to A. S. Suvorin, October 21, 1895, in *Pis'ma* [Letters], vol. 6 (Moscow: Nauka, 1978), 85.

30. Chekhov to M. P. Chekhov, October 18, 1896, in ibid., 197.

31. Chekhov to A. S. Suvorin, December 14, 1896, in ibid., 251.

Wood Demon in 1889, at least one member of the selection committee had been thrilled with Chekhov's novelistic play. The leading
St. Petersburg actor Pavel Svobodin praised Chekhov's "life-like
figures, living speech, and characters, which are beyond the whole
Alexandrinsky trash."[32] Similarly, despite the disastrous premiere
of *The Seagull*, at least one playwright saw something new and
exciting there too. When Vladimir Nemirovich-Danchenko won
the coveted Griboyedov Prize for drama in 1897, he said, "I told
the judges that [. . .] the prize should be given to *The Seagull*. [. . .]
The judges did not agree with me."[33] Chekhov's innovations, it
seemed, were not yet understood, let alone accepted, by the general
theatrical community.

Extremes of opinion soon traveled to the West. For every reviewer
who praised the 1914 production of *Uncle Vanya* in London, there
was one who reviled it. The play was either "an unforgettably good
play," or "desolate" and "dreary."[34]

Similarly, when the Moscow Art Theatre tours brought Chekhov
to the United States in 1923 and 1924,[35] argument continued
to rage. On one side sat audiences who wept in sympathy with
Chekhov's characters. During a performance of *Three Sisters,* an
actor described catching sight of a young woman who held the
play's translation in one hand and "in the other a handkerchief.
She cried, then quickly, quickly wiped away her tears, so that she
would not miss a word in the book, then again more tears."[36] On
the other side of the auditorium sat critics who argued that "the

---

32. Cited and translated by Ernest J. Simmons in *Chekhov: A Biography*
(Chicago: The University of Chicago Press, 1962), 198.

33. Vladimir Nemirovitch-Dantchenko [sic], *My Life in the Russian Theatre*
(Boston: Little, Brown, 1937), 71. (Note the old-fashioned and now uncom-
mon spelling of Nemirovich-Danchenko's name in this publication; I retain the
transliteration as published.)

34. Desmond MacCarthy and Egan Mew in Nick Worall, ed., *File on Chekhov*
(New York: Methuen, 1986), 48.

35. In 52 weeks, the Moscow Art Theatre gave 380 performances in the United
States, half of which were Chekhov's plays. See Sharon Marie Carnicke,
Stanislavsky in Focus: An Acting Master for the 21st Century, 2nd ed. (New
York: Routledge, 2008), chapter 2.

36. O. S. Bokshanskaya, "Iz perepiski s Vl. I. Nemirovichem-Danchenko
(Evropa i Amerika 1922–1924)" [Correspondence with Vl. I. Nemirovich-
Danchenko (Europe and America 1922–1924)], in *Ezhegodnik Moskovskogo
khudozhevstvennogo teatra: 1943* [The 1943 Yearbook of the Moscow Art
Theatre] (Moscow: MkhAT, 1945), 539.

plays of Chekhov, the very cornerstone upon which this admirable, this exemplary Moscow Art Theatre was builded, leave English-speaking peoples cold."[37] In the twenty-first century, the argument is still alive. For every one who makes Chekhov into her "new favorite writer,"[38] there is another who turns up his nose.

A Brief Life

When asked by Moscow University to provide an autobiography for his class reunion, Chekhov replied: "An autobiography? I have a disease: autobiographophobia. To read any details about myself genuinely torments me, and to write them for publication is even worse."[39] Scholars know a lot about Chekhov. He wrote an enormous number of letters, recording his daily life and registering his opinions. Yet, because he developed restraint and tact in his dealings with others, Chekhov the man still manages to elude us.

Biographers sometimes romanticize the facts of his life, creating novelistic stories about his rags-to-riches career, his love for the actress Olga Knipper, and his tragic death from tuberculosis at the age of forty-four. Biographers sometimes tackle, instead, the naked facts, assembling his complicated comings and goings, disentangling his friends from his acquaintances, and reconstructing his diverse activities and interests. Both types of biographies can lose sight of the forest for the trees. In the all-too-cursory account of Chekhov's life that follows, I point out those particular trees that best illuminate his writing of plays: his social background, his career in medicine, and his marriage to both the Moscow Art Theatre and the actress Olga Knipper.

The Blood of a Slave

On one rare occasion, Chekhov sent his editor a brief, yet accurate, autobiography, masked as an idea for a short story:

> What is free for writers born into the aristocracy comes at a high price for those born into the lower classes. The cost is their youth. Write a story about a young man,

37. Corbin, review of *Three Sisters*, 241.

38. Sarah Boots, Freshman Seminar: Checking Out Chekhov, University of Southern California, Fall 2008.

39. Chekhov to G. I. Rossiolimo, October 11, 1899, in *Pis'ma* [Letters], vol. 8 (Moscow: Nauka, 1980), 284.

the son of a serf, a former shopkeeper, singer [in the
church choir], school-boy and university student, raised
with respect for rank, kissing the hands of priests, bow-
ing to others' ideas, grateful for every piece of bread,
beaten many times, going to school without galoshes,
picking fights, tormenting animals, loving dinners with
rich relatives, playing the hypocrite with both God and
people because he thought himself good for nothing.
Write about how this young man presses the slave out
of himself drop by drop, and how he awakens one fine
morning and feels he no longer has the blood of a slave
in his veins, but that of a real human being.[40]

Anton Pavlovich Chekhov was born on January 16, 1860, in
Taganrog;[41] he was the third oldest son in a family of five boys and
two girls. For the next forty-four years he celebrated his birthday
on January 17, the day dedicated to St. Anthony, for whom he
was named. His native city was a provincial capital in southern
Russia near the Ukraine, with a cosmopolitan population because
of its port (where Greek merchants traded) and its military base.
His family's background reflected Russia's past. Like Lopakhin's
father in *The Cherry Orchard,* Anton's father, Pavel, had been born
into serfdom, Russia's form of slavery. When Pavel reached age
nineteen, his father, Yegor (Anton's grandfather), had somehow
amassed enough money to buy his and his family's freedom from
their owner, Count Chertkov.[42]

Pavel Chekhov owned a small shop that sold groceries, sundries,
and even medicines (most of them quack preparations). He was especially proud of having joined the merchant guild because it raised
his class status, as measured by the Russian government, by two
ranks above the free peasants. He was ambitious for his sons, and
thus insured that they learn to respect authority, pay strict attention
to church doctrine, and get a solid education (grounded in foreign
languages, including Latin and Greek). As choir director for the

40. Chekhov to A. S. Suvorin, January 7, 1889, in *Pis'ma* [Letters], vol. 3,
133.

41. All biographical dates are given according to the Julian calendar, which
was used in Russia during Chekhov's life; dates are therefore twelve days earlier than in the Gregorian calendar, used elsewhere.

42. Yegor Chekhov had accumulated only enough to buy his sons' freedom;
Chertkov took pity on him and included Yegor's daughter for free.

local churches, Pavel also demanded that his children dedicate themselves to liturgical music. They sang in church every morning. Anton would later use this training to create uniquely musical plays.

Given Pavel's roots as a serf, he also expected hard work from his children. Anton tended the store whenever he was not in school or with the choir; his day began at five o'clock in the morning in church and ended at midnight in the store. Even the slightest infraction of the rules meant a physical beating from Pavel. As Chekhov once said, "There was no childhood in my childhood."[43]

In 1876, Pavel Chekhov went bankrupt; he lost his store and his membership in the merchant guild. He dropped in status to one rung above the peasants. With no income, Pavel escaped from debtors' prison by leaving town in the dead of night with most of his family. At sixteen Anton was left behind to finish school; the rest of his family resettled in the slums of Moscow. Alone in Taganrog, Anton tried but failed to fend off his father's creditors. It was he who watched his family's house and furniture sold to their former tenant, a civil servant with a penchant for gambling. Echoes of this period find their way into his plays, as in *The Cherry Orchard* when a family loses their home to their former serf.

The Moscow Art Theatre production of *The Cherry Orchard,* 1904. This photograph, taken in 1915, shows Olga Knipper (as Lyubov Ranevskaya) and Konstantin Stanislavsky (as Gayev) standing in the center of the group to the left and Chekhov's nephew, Michael Chekhov (as Yepikhodov), standing in the background near the door.

43. As cited and translated by Simmons, *Chekhov,* 6.

Chekhov's difficult upbringing taught him restraint. "I am short-tempered, etc., etc.," he later told his wife, "but I have gotten used to holding myself back, because letting oneself go doesn't suit a decent person."[44] Moreover, by "pressing the slave out of himself drop by drop," he developed a lifelong dedication to freedom and fairness.

> I am not a liberal, not a conservative, not an evolutionist, not a monk, but neither am I indifferent. I would like to be a free artist, and I only fear that God has not given me the strength to become one. I hate lies and coercion in any form. [. . .] My holy of holies is the human body, health, the mind, talent, inspiration, love, and the most absolute freedom, freedom from coercion and lies, in whatever ways these might be expressed.[45]

A "Medicle" Career

Anton graduated from high school in 1879 with grades that earned him a scholarship to Moscow University, where he studied medicine. He later recalled that "when I applied for entrance, I wrote down 'medicle' school" in error.[46] Perhaps Anton chose medicine as his career because he had seen desperately ill peasants buying quack medicines at his father's store. Perhaps he hoped to cure the many members of his family who were ill with tuberculosis. In reflecting on two family deaths from this widespread disease, Chekhov wrote, "The trouble is that both these deaths (A. and N.) are not an accident, and not an event in human life, but an ordinary thing."[47] Whatever the motivation, Chekhov devoted himself to medicine his whole life, often calling it "my lawful wife." Literature was "my mistress."[48]

---

44. Chekhov to O. L. Knipper, February 11, 1903, in *Pis'ma* [Letters], vol. 11, 150.

45. Chekhov to A. N. Pleshcheyev, October 4, 1888, in *Pis'ma* [Letters], vol. 3, 10.

46. Chekhov to G. I. Rossiolimo, October 11, 1899, in *Pis'ma* [Letters], vol. 8, 284.

47. An 1891 notebook entry, cited and translated by Rayfield, *Anton Chekhov*, 322.

48. See, for example, letters by Chekhov on January 17, 1887, in *Pis'ma* [Letters], vol. 2, 14; on February 11, 1893, *Pis'ma* [Letters], vol. 5 (Moscow: Nauka, 1977), 169; and on March 15, 1896, in *Pis'ma* [Letters], vol. 6, 132.

In moving to Moscow for medical school, Anton also became the de facto head of a large, woefully dependent, and largely dysfunctional family. His father had at last found menial work as a clerk, but his two elder brothers were in trouble. Alexander (an intelligent writer) had become an alcoholic; Nikolay (a gifted visual artist and illustrator) was suffering from tuberculosis and was addicted to the treatments of morphine.

It was now up to Anton to pay the rent, buy the food, and make sure his younger siblings finished school. There is little doubt that his prodigious writing during the 1880s provided significant and necessary additional income. His hasty writing reflects the fact that he was paid per line; the more lines he could write the more money he could earn for his family. When his level-headed younger sister, Masha, graduated as a school teacher, she became Anton's right hand, managing the household for him whenever medicine and literature called him away.

Upon graduation in 1884, Dr. Chekhov opened his practice in Moscow. He was already showing early symptoms of the family's disease. When Nikolay died on January 17, 1889 (Anton's nameday), the young doctor fell into a deep depression that he handled in an extraordinary way. In April 1890 he undertook a massive scientific study of Russia's most notorious penal colony, Sakhalin, in the Far East. He traveled eighty-one days by horse, rail, and steamship through storms and the cold of Siberia to get to the remote island prison; the grueling journey clearly affected his health and may have accelerated his death. Once in Sakhalin, he spent eight months processing questionnaires for 10,000 convicts and their families, all exiled for life. He conducted as many as 160 interviews daily, amassing information and statistics previously unknown to Russia's government. When he returned home, he exposed the reality of Russia's penal system in his book *The Island of Sakhalin* (1891) and began a fund-raising campaign to send books to the convicts' children.

By 1892 Chekhov had earned enough money to buy a tumbledown country estate called Melikhovo, located forty-five miles by train outside Moscow and six more miles by horse on muddy roads from the railroad station. In buying this estate, Chekhov may well have wanted to escape the cruelties of human behavior (which he had so starkly confronted at Sakhalin) and find peace in nature. Melikhovo consisted of 600 acres of birch forests, pastures, and farmland. Chekhov also planted flowers and a cherry orchard of his own, which no doubt provided inspiration for his last play. Yet, life was not easy at Melikhovo. The dilapidated house was large but had no bathroom or insulation. He and Masha struggled to make the orchard and farm productive. Chekhov lived at his estate from 1892 until 1899, when his deteriorating health made a move to warmer climates essential. During this time, Chekhov also worked as the area's doctor, becoming solely responsible for the health of twenty-six surrounding villages and seven factories.

Over the years, Chekhov's civic work included fund-raising for the victims of Russia's famine in 1891, volunteering as a doctor during the cholera epidemic in 1892, and building three schools for peasants in the villages around Melikhovo and a sanatorium for tuberculosis near the city of Yalta on the Black Sea (where he would eventually move). These endeavors earned him a national award, the Stanislaus Medal (third class) in 1899.[49]

Chekhov's knowledge as a doctor must have made facing his own illness especially difficult. He used a lot of ink in letters to explain away the periodic bleeding from his lungs. He strenuously resisted allowing another doctor to examine him. Over the years he made light of his illness in letters to his siblings and to his wife. Yet, he could hardly hold any illusions about his diagnosis. He had suffered recognizable symptoms of tuberculosis throughout medical school, and in 1894 he joked with a friend that he would live only five or ten more years. In 1897 a serious hemorrhage from the lungs hospitalized him; he could no longer deny the truth. He sold Melikhovo and built a new house in the warmer climate of Yalta.

Chekhov wrote *The Cherry Orchard* during 1903 when he was very ill. Thus, the work was painfully slow. Interrupted by bouts of coughing, diarrhea, an inability to eat, and depression, he struggled to keep writing. Whereas writing had once flowed easily from him, now he could write only a line or two a day. "There is still weakness and coughing," he told his wife, but "I write everyday; although only a little, still I write."[50] At times, he felt despair. "I am beginning to lose heart. It seems to me that I have outlived my time as a writer, and that every sentence I write seems to serve no purpose, and no need whatever."[51] Despite his condition, he forged ahead, promising that his "last act will be merry, and indeed the whole play will be

49. Rayfield, *Anton Chekhov*, 507.

50. Chekhov to O. L. Knipper, October 2, 1903, in *Pis'ma* [Letters], vol. 11, 260.

51. Chekhov to O. L. Knipper, September 20, 1903, in ibid., 252.

light and merry."[52] Finally in October he sent the play to the Moscow Art Theatre, telling his wife that he was pleased with the result. He worried only that "I did not write in one sitting, but over a long, very long time, and so it will probably seem somehow drawn out." He added, "Darling, how hard it was for me to write the play!"[53]

In 1904 he risked one last trip to Moscow, appearing on January 17 (his name-day) for the premiere of *The Cherry Orchard*. He arrived at the Moscow Art Theatre just before the last act and was promptly called to the stage by loud applause. He was emaciated, pale, and hardly able to stand on stage as the company made speeches in his honor.[54] By spring, his condition turned mortal. On the advice of Muscovite doctors, his wife rushed him to the German health spa of Badenweiler. But the trip itself was dangerous for him. He died in the warmth of the resort on July 2, 1904. He is buried in Moscow's Novodevichy cemetery.

Chekhov's medical point of view is everywhere visible in his plays. He invites us to diagnose the ills of his characters' souls in precisely the same way that doctors diagnose physical illnesses—by observing the outward symptoms closely. In *The Cherry Orchard*, Lyubov's addiction to coffee and pills suggests her persistent heartache, and Gayev's obsession with imaginary games of billiards demonstrates his desire to escape reality.

In addition, good doctors treat their patients without judging their morals. So, too, does Chekhov examine his characters' outward symptoms, leaving all moralizing aside. Consider the following letter in which Chekhov defends his primary technique to his editor:

> You upbraid me for my objectivity, calling it an indifference to good and evil [. . .]. You want me, when I depict horse-thieves, to say: stealing horses is evil. But surely, everyone knows that without my saying so. Let a jury judge them; my business is only to show them as they are. [. . . As I write,] I must speak and think in their tones of voice, I must feel as they do [. . .]. When I write, I rely on my readers, I assume that they will fill in the subjective elements in my story.[55]

52. Chekhov to O. L. Knipper, September 21, 1903, in ibid., 253.

53. Chekhov to O. L. Knipper, October 12, 1903, in ibid., 271.

54. Rayfield, *Anton Chekhov*, 587.

55. Chekhov to A. S. Suvorin, April 1, 1890, in *Pis'ma* [Letters], vol. 4 (Moscow: Nauka, 1976), 54.

If we expect a play to illuminate the ills of society or to teach us how to live, then Chekhov's plays do indeed seem wanting. If, however, we understand that our job as the audience is to pay attention to the characters and "fill in the subjective elements,"[56] then Chekhov's plays become endlessly fascinating.

Marriage to the Moscow Art Theatre

Beginning in 1898 with a radically innovative production of *The Seagull* directed by Konstantin Stanislavsky, the Moscow Art Theatre[57] turned Chekhov into a world-famous playwright. Not only did Russian theater audiences see Chekhov through the eyes of the Muscovite company, but so did European and American spectators. First in 1906, and then in 1923 to 1924, the Art Theatre took their Chekhov productions on tour. In many cases, their Russian-language performances were Chekhov premieres in the United States. No wonder that Chekhov's name will be forever linked to that of Stanislavsky and the Moscow Art Theatre.

With Chekhov's marriage in 1901 to Olga Knipper, a founding member of the Moscow Art Theatre, he forged more than a professional link with the company. He had first admired Knipper's acting in 1897. She then took note of him during rehearsals for *The Seagull,* in which she played the leading role of Arkadina. In April 1899, mutual interest turned into a serious relationship and then marriage. However, because she performed on the Moscow stage while he remained in Yalta for his health, they were often apart. This fate meant that thousands of letters between them document their love.

While Chekhov did not need the Art Theatre to become a famous writer, he did need it to become an influential dramatist. In return, Chekhov offered precisely what the company's cofounders needed: the financial stability that comes with sold-out houses and innovative writing that could make their theatrical ideals stunningly visible. His colloquial language, sound effects taken from daily life, and tightly knit groups of characters were in close sympathy with the company's goals.

---

56. Ibid.

57. This company, arguably the most important theatrical enterprise in the twentieth century, was the breeding ground for the now globally famous Stanislavsky System of actor training. For more information, see Carnicke, *Stanislavsky in Focus.*

The Moscow Art Theatre was founded on June 22, 1897, when Stanislavsky and Nemirovich-Danchenko met for dinner at the Slavic Bazaar Hotel. In a now-legendary eighteen-hour meeting, Stanislavsky and Nemirovich-Danchenko laid down the principles of their innovative theater. At thirty-three, Konstantin Sergeyevich Alekseyev had been acting for twenty years under the stage name Stanislavsky. His fresh talent had caught Nemirovich-Danchenko's eye. At thirty-nine, Vladimir Ivanovich Nemirovich-Danchenko was a theater critic, a member of the Repertory Committee of the Imperial Theatres, and a successful playwright. In 1891 Nemirovich-Danchenko had become director of a professional actor-training program in Moscow, the Philharmonic Society's Drama School.

Appalled by the artificiality of professional acting, insufficient rehearsal time, poor standards of scenic design, and lack of respect for the playwright, Nemirovich-Danchenko had begun to dream of a way "to reconstruct [theater's] whole life [. . .] to change at the root the whole order of rehearsals and the preparation of plays; to subject the public itself to the regime essential to our purpose."[58] He had invited Stanislavsky to dinner to see whether they might together reform Moscow's theatrical practice. As they laid down a plan for their new theater, Stanislavsky called it nothing less than "revolutionary":

> We protested against the old manner of acting, against theatricality, against false pathos, declamation, against overacting, against the bad conventions of production and design, against the star system which spoils the ensemble, against the whole construct of the spectacle and against the unsubstantial repertoire of past theatres.[59]

Each partner brought a special angle of vision to the enterprise. As a writer, Nemirovich-Danchenko understood that a play's "main idea" could be used to construct the "scaffolding" for a unified production. As an actor, Stanislavsky put "human life into that scaffolding."[60]

58. Nemirovitch-Dantchenko [sic], *My Life in the Russian Theatre*, 68.

59. K. S. Stanislavsky, *Sobranie sochinenii* [Collected Works], vol. 1 (Moscow: Iskusstvo, 1988), 254.

60. Michael Chekhov, "Lecture 10: Experience at the Moscow Art Theatre," audio-taped lecture (Hollywood, 1955) in The New York Public Library for the Performing Arts.

"You must fall in love!" Lyubov Andreyevna (played by Olga Knipper) to Trofimov (played by Vassily Kachalov) in *The Cherry Orchard,* The Moscow Art Theatre 1904.

One basic attitude links all points in their program for theatrical reform: respect for theater as art, not mere entertainment. On stage, all theatrical elements would support a central conceptual approach to the play. "Poet, actor, designer, tailor, and stage-hand all work toward one goal, set down by the poet in the foundation of the play."[61] In regard to design, sets were no longer assembled from furniture in stock, but were built to express the play's overarching idea. Similarly, unmatched clothes provided by actors were replaced with costumes designed to further the production as an integrated whole.[62] Nemirovich-Danchenko and Stanislavsky even dared to reform their audiences. They put chairs in the auditorium that were not very comfortable in order to insure their spectators' lively attention. They also banned disrespectful late arrivals and applause that might inappropriately interrupt the flow of the play.

In regard to acting, the cofounders expected actors to craft characters that served the play, not to show virtuosity for its own sake.

61. Stanislavsky, *Sobranie sochinenii* [Collected Works], vol. 1, 250.

62. In *The Seagull,* the actress Arkadina complains that she cannot afford to buy her son a new suit because she must provide her own costumes. She alludes to one of the many realities in professional theater, which the Moscow Art Theatre successfully reformed.

Hence, Nemirovich-Danchenko and Stanislavsky banished stars from their company. "Today—Hamlet, tomorrow—an extra, but even as an extra—an artist. [. . .] There are no small roles, only small actors."[63] Stars may have performed in *The Seagull* at the Alexandrinsky Theatre, but artists filled its roles at the Moscow Art. This attitude toward acting meant that actors had to work together as a cooperative ensemble, like musicians in a well-tuned orchestra. Each instrument contributes to the symphony. Such an orchestra of actors admirably suited Chekhov's plays, where all characters are equally vivid.

By 1898 the Moscow Art Theatre had opened to critical acclaim, but it was struggling financially. Nemirovich-Danchenko realized that *The Seagull*, with its innovative structure and a leading character who calls for "new forms" in theatrical art, would be perfect for their company. Moreover, Nemirovich-Danchenko realized that Chekhov's apparent failure as a playwright had less to do with the author's ignorance of stage convention and more to do with standard productions that did not support his fresh conception of drama. For example, the first production of Chekhov's *Ivanov* (1889) "left not a trace in the theatre because there was nothing strictly 'Chekhovian' about it. [. . . For this production,] the favorite actors had scored a success: it was pleasant to see them again in other attire and in other make-up,"[64] and that was all. In short, Chekhov suffered from routine success. As Nemirovich-Danchenko writes of the 1897 premiere of Chekhov's *Uncle Vanya* in the Ukrainian city of Odessa:

> The public applauded, the actors were called before the curtain, but with the end of the performance came also the end of the play's life; the spectators did not bear away with them any intensely lived experience; the play did not awaken them to a new understanding of things. I repeat: there was nothing of that new reflection of life which a new poet had brought to his play.[65]

In April 1898 Nemirovich-Danchenko began an aggressive campaign to persuade Chekhov to give the Moscow Art Theatre permission to stage *The Seagull*. But Chekhov was unwilling; he

---

63. Stanislavsky, *Sobranie sochinenii* [Collected Works], vol. 1, 250.
64. Nemirovitch-Dantchenko [sic], *My Life in the Russian Theatre*, 22–23.
65. Ibid., 50.

was still deeply pained by its St. Petersburg premiere. Nemirovich-Danchenko argued that "a conscientious production" of *The Seagull* "without banalities will thrill the audience." He promised Chekhov just such a production. "Perhaps the play won't get bursts of applause, but a real production with *fresh* talents, *free of routine*, will be a triumph of art, I guarantee that."[66] Chekhov relented in June, and in September Stanislavsky began to direct the play in consultation with his partner.

The Moscow Art Theatre production opened on December 17, 1898, after a record number of twenty-four regular and three dress rehearsals; the company was not yet confident in their work. Nemirovich-Danchenko vividly recalls the tense mood backstage as the first act curtain closed:

> There was a silence, a complete silence both in the theatre and on the stage, it was as though all held their breath, as though no one quite understood [what they had seen . . .]. This mood lasted quite a long time, so long indeed that those on stage decided that the first act had failed, failed so completely that not a single friend in the audience dared applaud. [. . .] Then suddenly, in the auditorium something happened. It was as if a dam had burst, or a bomb had exploded—all at once there was a deafening crash of applause from all: from friends and from enemies.[67]

The performance had made theatrical history, and, to this day, a simple sketch of a seagull brands the Moscow Art Theatre's work.

At the outset, theatrical reform at the Moscow Art Theatre meant bringing the best of European stage realism to Russia. Hence, the company staged Chekhov's plays with great attention to realistic detail. Three-dimensional sets that looked like real rooms with the fourth wall removed gave audiences the sense that they were eavesdropping on the lives of real people. Realistic props and historically accurate costumes further anchored the play to reality. In fact, Stanislavsky insisted that the actors begin using props and costumes as early as two months before the premiere of each play

---

66. Vladimir Nemirovich-Danchenko, letter to A. P. Chekhov, April 25, 1898, in *Tvorcheskoe nasledie* [Creative Legacy], vol. I (Moscow: Moskovskii khudozhestvennyi teatr, 2003), 165–66; the italics are Nemirovich-Danchenko's.

67. Nemirovitch-Dantchenko [sic], *My Life in the Russian Theatre*, 187–88.

in order to induce their imaginative belief in Chekhov's world.[68] Stanislavsky also added a great number of production effects in lighting and sound to stimulate further the actors' imaginations. In his 1904 production plan for *The Cherry Orchard*, for example, he ends Act I with a plethora of sounds: "A shepherd plays on his pipe, the neighing of horses, the mooing of cows, the bleating of sheep and the lowing of cattle are heard."[69] Stanislavsky exceeded his European models, however, by melding realism in design with extraordinarily credible acting. Initially, he created three-dimensionality in actors through purely physical and technical means.[70] He carefully directed their movements to create an illusion of truth. Actors appeared oblivious of the audience; they spoke to each other, not to spectators. Sometimes they even turned their backs on the auditorium, as they did in *The Seagull* to watch Treplev's play-within-the-play. When the Moscow Art Theatre toured the United States, critics often commented on precisely this aspect of the actors' work in Chekhov's plays. For example, after viewing *The Cherry Orchard*, Edmund Wilson wrote: "[We watch] the family go about its business [. . .] without anything which we recognize as theatrical, but with the brightness of the highest art."[71]

Following the success of *The Seagull*, the Moscow Art Theatre naturally assumed that Chekhov had joined them. But, unbeknownst to the company, Chekhov had submitted *Uncle Vanya* to their competitor, the Maly Theatre. Only when the Maly rejected it did Chekhov decide to place his fate squarely in Stanislavsky's and Nemirovich-Danchenko's hands. He wrote his last two plays, *Three Sisters* and *The Cherry Orchard*, with the Moscow Art Theatre actors specifically in mind.

In *The Cherry Orchard*, Stanislavsky's acting created an especially memorable performance. His final exit as Gayev became an emotional high point in the premiere production. The orchard has been sold; all the bags have been packed; the members of the household are rushing to get to their trains; only the two landowners

---

68. Ibid., 100.

69. K. S. Stanislavsky, *Rezhisserskie ekzempliary K. S. Stanislavskogom* [Directorial Plans of K. S. Stanislavsky], vol. 3 (Moscow: Iskusstvo, 1983), 337.

70. Only after Chekhov's death would Stanislavsky begin to develop his system of actor training. See Carnicke, *Stanislavsky in Focus*.

71. Edmund Wilson, review of *The Cherry Orchard*, *Dial*, January 1923 in Emeljanow, ed., *Chekhov: The Critical Heritage*, 236.

remain on stage. When Gayev turns to speak to his sister, she too has left without his noticing. Alone on stage:

> He is about to break into violent sobbing when suddenly he stuffs his handkerchief in his mouth like a schoolboy caught laughing. As he turns his back and goes out we see the twitch of the big shoulders and it is almost more than an impressionable playgoer can bear.[72]

Many years afterward, this moment haunted the American director Harold Clurman: "I shall never forget the heartbreak—not without its humour—when Stanislavsky, as Gayev in the original production, reached ineffectually for his handkerchief."[73] In this moment, Stanislavsky clearly embodied his initial view of the play as emotionally tragic.

A close look at Chekhov's plays makes sense of his equivocation with the Theatre's staging of them. Chekhov does indeed use daily

The Moscow Art Theatre production of *The Cherry Orchard,* 1904. This photograph shows the last moment of the play with the Act I nursery (see p. xxiii) now stripped of all furnishings and Firs (played by Alexander Artem) lying on the sofa to the left. Billy Rose Theatre Division, The New York Public Library for the Performing Arts, Astor, Lenox and Tilden Foundations.

72. Heywood Broun, "The New Plays," *New York World,* January 23, 1923, Clippings, The New York Public Library, Performing Arts Research Collections, New York.

73. Harold Clurman, *The Naked Image: Observations on the Modern Theatre* (New York: Collier-Macmillan Ltd., 1966), 284.

life and colloquial speech to bring his characters to life, and he does indeed provide psychological insights into human behavior, but he does not actually write realistic plays. He carefully selects details from life to express more than surface reality. Wilson recognized this aspect of Chekhov's art when he wrote that the actors of the Moscow Art Theatre "bring out a whole set of aesthetic values to which we are not accustomed in the realistic theater: the beauty and poignancy of an atmosphere, of an idea, a person, a moment are caught, and put before us without emphasis."[74] In this selectivity, Chekhov was influenced by symbolists like the Belgian playwright Maurice Maeterlinck (1862–1949).

Read any of Maeterlinck's short plays from the 1890s, such as *The Intruder* (about a family who sits together through the night waiting for the arrival of Death) or *The Seven Princesses* (a nightmarish fairy tale), and you will better understand Chekhov. Maeterlinck repeats sentences to suggest the depths of human experience behind even the simplest of statements. He uses eerie images and sounds to create transcendental atmospheres. Chekhov, too, uses patterns of repeated dialogue, images, and sounds in all his plays, but nowhere is there a more Maeterlinckian moment than in *The Cherry Orchard*. In Act II, during a desultory conversation, the characters suddenly fall silent. At just that moment a mysterious sound is heard; it is something like the snapping of a string, or the call of an owl, or a bucket falling in an underground mine shaft. This sound is heard again, like a symbolist refrain, when the curtain falls at the end of the play. As Firs—old, ill, forgotten by the others, and locked accidentally inside the empty house—lies down to wait for someone to find him (or perhaps to die), the same mysterious sound is heard again. This time it is set against the mundane sounds of axes chopping down the orchard. Does Chekhov now make clear that this sound is a death knell?

Despite Chekhov's attraction to symbolism, however, he rejected the movement's interest in total abstraction. Treplev's play in *The Seagull* is a brilliant parody of a symbolist drama that has lost its moorings in reality. Thus, while Maeterlinck draws his refrains from the abstract world of poetic imagery, Chekhov transforms the details of ordinary life into poetic images.[75] The sound of death in *The Cherry Orchard* may be otherworldly, but it also may be just

---

74. Wilson, review of *The Cherry Orchard*, 236.

75. For more on this topic, see Laurence Senelick, "Chekhov's Drama, Maeterlinck, and the Russian Symbolists," in Jean-Pierre Baricelli, ed.,

the call of an owl or the falling of a bucket in a mine shaft somewhere far away.

No wonder Chekhov found the Moscow Art Theatre's love of realism so problematic! Production effects threatened to dilute and thereby hide his careful selection of expressive details. At a rehearsal of *The Seagull,* Chekhov was overheard asking: "'Why all these details?' [. . .] 'But it's realistic!' he heard in reply, to which Chekhov ironically remarked that a living nose taken from the model for a portrait and placed on the spot of the painted one is also realistic."[76] Annoyed, Chekhov threatened to write the following opening line for his next play: "How wonderful, how quiet! Not a bird, a dog, a cuckoo, an owl, a nightingale, or clocks, or jingling bells, not even one cricket to be heard."[77]

The Devil in the Details

While Chekhov's innovations in drama illuminate much about *The Cherry Orchard,* one needs also to examine his play through a microscope to fully understand his dramatic flair. The devil, they say, is in the details, and so it is with Chekhov.

During rehearsals for his second major play, *Uncle Vanya,* Chekhov criticized Stanislavsky for assuming that the title character wears boots and work clothes simply because he manages the estate. "'Listen,' [Chekhov] said getting annoyed, 'everything is written down. You haven't read the play.'" Stanislavsky searched through the text but could find nothing more than an apparently off-hand comment about a "stylish tie." When the puzzled director asked the author to explain, Chekhov said, Vanya "has a wonderful tie; he is an elegant, cultured man. It's not true, that all landowners go around in muddy boots. They are educated people, they dress well, they go to Paris. I wrote all that."[78] This anecdote demonstrates how important the smallest item, like a "stylish tie," could be to

Chekhov's Great Plays: A Critical Anthology (New York: New York University Press, 1981), 161–80.

76. V. E. Meyerhold, *O Teatre* [About Theatre] (St. Petersburg: Prosveshchenie, 1913), 24.

77. Jean Benedetti, *Stanislavski: A Biography* (New York: Routledge, 1990), 135.

78. Stanislavsky, *Sobranie sochinenii* [Collected Works], vol. 1, 300.

Chekhov the playwright. It also suggests how closely he expected directors and actors to read his plays.

One of the pleasures in translating Chekhov involves paying close attention to him. The work of rendering Russian into English reveals the threads that make up the fabric of his plays. Only in a close, close reading can one see Chekhov's precision. Nothing, not one word, is irrelevant to the whole. This tightly woven fabric is what allows readers and audiences to revisit Chekhov's plays time after time, always finding something new within them.

I now invite you to enter *The Cherry Orchard* more deeply by focusing your eyes and attuning your ears to the kinds of devilish details that Chekhov loves. Discussion of some of these follows.

1. Clothing as Commentary

As Vanya's stylish tie suggests, clothes in a Chekhov play often comment upon the characters. When the curtain opens on *The Cherry Orchard,* spectators see a man dressed in an elegant white waistcoat and expensive but gaudy yellow shoes; he seems a fine gentleman who flaunts his wealth. A well-dressed and perfectly coifed woman then enters to join him; she seems his match. Their apparel suggests that they might well be the owners of the cherry orchard, but their words soon belie their clothes. Lopakhin feels that, however fine his clothes, he is still an uneducated peasant underneath. "You can't make a silk purse out of a sow's ear," he says. Then eying Dunyasha's fashionable appearance, he brusquely observes that she should dress like the servant she is. "You ought to remember your place," he tells her.

Chekhov has begun his play with a visual sleight of hand, as deft as the card tricks that Charlotta (a former circus performer) will later use to entertain her masters. Through Lopakhin's and Dunyasha's inappropriate clothing, Chekhov expresses their upwardly mobile aspirations and also warns his audience that all is not always what it seems.

Chekhov continues to play with clothing and social roles throughout the play. If Lopakhin wishes to overcome his peasant roots by donning expensive clothes, how can he then marry a woman like Varya, who chooses to dress below her station? As the landowner's adopted daughter, she might well don Dunyasha's fancy dress, but instead Varya chooses the dour clothes of a servant, with keys hanging at her waist like a nun's rosary. Indeed, she looks, we're told by her mother, "like a nun." Similarly, if Dunyasha aspires to a lady's delicacy of feelings by putting on the latest fashion and primping her hair, then how can she agree to marry the oaf, Yepikhodov,[79] who lacks all style? No wonder Dunyasha prefers the dandified cad, Yasha, who so drenches himself in patchouli (the latest French perfume) that people can tell when he has been in a room by the smell.

Moreover, Chekhov's playful use of inappropriate clothing alerts his astute spectators to other discrepancies. For example, before the play begins, the seventeen-year-old Anya has travelled to Paris to fetch her runaway mother. Despite news of the impending auction and numerous pleading telegrams, Lyubov kept delaying her return until finally escorted home by her daughter. In short, the child plays the role of the parent to her errant mother. Similarly, when their home is finally sold at auction, the child comforts and reassures her parent, again turning audience expectations inside out. While Anya and her mother are appropriately dressed, they have exchanged behavioral roles as surely as Dunyasha and Varya have exchanged dresses.

2. Apparent Non Sequiturs in Conversations and Behavior

Sometimes conversation in a Chekhov play seems comedic because it appears to flow illogically. One famous example of a non sequitur in *The Cherry Orchard* is Charlotta's entrance line, "My dog eats nuts." While irrelevant to the onstage action, her words presumably make sense in terms of the offstage conversation that is in progress when she enters. Chekhov does nothing new here; Shakespeare used the same technique to make his plays seem as continuous as real life.

But occasionally, Chekhov has more insidious strategies in mind. He also uses non sequiturs to comment on the wider action of a scene. For example, in the last act of *The Cherry Orchard,* Anya is comforting her mother: "Mama, you'll come back soon, soon . . . Isn't that true? [. . .] Mama, you'll come back . . ." Lyubov, in turn, reassures her daughter with a hug: "I'll come back, my precious." Next Charlotta decides to perform a feat of ventriloquism, which seems inappropriately timed. She "picks up a bundle and holds it to look like a baby wrapped in a blanket." The baby cries, and Charlotta comforts the imaginary child with "I'm so sorry for you!" Then she abruptly "throws the bundle down." In effect, Anya's

---

79. Yepikhodov's name derives from the Russian verb *khodit'*, "to walk," but, being accident prone, he trips more often than he walks.

governess has just criticized the lack of maternal feeling in Lyubov by debunking her motherly reassurance.

Then again, Chekhov sometimes uses non sequiturs to suggest new levels of meaning within his play. For example, whenever Firs answers questions illogically because he is hard of hearing, we might laugh, but we also might come to understand that clear communication between people is always difficult. In some sense, we are all hard of hearing.

3. Apparent Irrelevancies

Details that appear irrelevant can function as creatively as non sequiturs do in Chekhov's world. Take another look at Gayev's constant and apparently irrelevant references to billiards. As noted before, his on-going, imaginary game functions as a physical symptom of his psychological state of mind. But Gayev's obsession with billiards is also more than this; it provides a significant image for Chekhov's handling of action throughout the play.

Characters in *The Cherry Orchard* tend to avoid direct confrontations with each other, preferring to step away from fights. Thus, open conflicts are rare in Chekhov's plays generally. Furthermore, over the course of his career, he tended to write fewer and fewer scenes in which conflict takes center stage. *The Cherry Orchard* represents the pinnacle of this trend in his writing. Central to the play are Lopakhin's two attempts to persuade Lyubov to build summer houses in order to save her estate from auction and Lyubov's two attempts to persuade Lopakhin to propose to Varya. In all four scenes, persuasion is met by indirect rebuttal. When confronted by Lopakhin about the auction, Lyubov changes the subject. In Act I, she appears to engage with Lopakhin for a moment but then quickly drifts off into remarks about Paris. In Act II, when Lopakhin demands that she "answer in one word," she immediately deflects him: "Who's been smoking those revolting cigars here . . ." When Lyubov raises the idea of marriage to Varya, Lopakhin's mode of rebuttal is different but still indirect. He always agrees with Lyubov, but so half-heartedly that it is difficult to take him at his word. In Act II, he says: "Well? I'm not against it . . . She's a good girl." In Act IV, he even agrees when Lyubov tells him that she doesn't understand why he has not yet proposed: "I have to admit I don't understand it either," he says.

Their interactions with each other have become a game of indirection that mirrors the game of angles in billiards. Rarely does a billiards' player use the cue ball to hit his actual target square on;

instead, he reaches his target by hitting a by-standing ball that sets a number of other balls into motion until the target is reached and a point is finally scored. Events do occur in Chekhov. Lyubov loses her orchard and returns to her lover in Paris; Lopakhin loses Varya and buys the cherry orchard. Yet these events come about in much the same way that billiard balls score points—through indirection—leaving characters feeling side-swiped and audiences wondering what the characters' actual targets of desire really were all along.

4. Puns, Verbal Tics, Eccentric Grammar, and Meaningless Phrases

Chekhov delights in word play of all kinds. For example, he uses a pun when Lyubov asks Gayev to lend money to their neighbor for his mortgage debt. "Give it to him, Leonid," she says. He ironically answers, "I'll give it to him all right!" His punning answer also echoes Varya's earlier comment on Lopakhin's maddening passivity toward her: "If only I could give it to him . . ."

Chekhov also gives his characters distinctive ways of speaking that can tell us as much about them as does their clothing. Sometimes Chekhov gives them verbal tics, as in Gayev's continual use of billiards' jargon. Sometimes characters use distorted grammar, revealing their intellectual ambitions and their flaws. Yepikhodov often speaks ungrammatically, getting tangled up in long, convoluted sentences and big, elegant, but incorrectly used, words; his speech alone marks him as one of Chekhov's clowns. If something in my translation strikes you as peculiar in English, know that it is also peculiar in Russian.

My favorite instance of word play in *The Cherry Orchard* is Firs' devilishly untranslatable word, *nedotyópa*. He mutters it whenever he criticizes Dunyasha and Yasha for their flightiness; Lyubov quotes it when she reprimands Trofimov for not acting like a grown-up; and Chekhov uses it as the very last word in the play when Firs lies down in the empty house. Some scholars think the word might be Ukrainian for "incompetent." Some think that it is slang that Chekhov heard while working as a doctor in Russia's provinces. Russian dictionaries from the 1930s cite Chekhov as its originator.[80] Translators have rendered it in many different ways: "good for nothing," "addle pate," "job-lot," "pathetic old fool," "you old fool," "flibbertigibbet," and "sillybilly." My solution is

---

80. Laurence Senelick, *Anton Chekhov* (New York: Grove Press, 1985), 133–34.

"nincompoop,"[81] because it picks up the Russian word's nonsensical quality as well as its percussive sound.

5. Grandiloquent Speech and Philosophizing

While it is tempting to take the beautiful passages in Chekhov's plays as genuinely poetic riffs on life, the careful reader may also begin to suspect that sometimes philosophy reveals the underbellies of would-be heroes. Talk, in and of itself, can hide a character's flaws.

For instance, Trofimov waxes poetic about Russia's genuine need for revolutionary reform, and because history would later prove him right, he seems prophetic. No wonder interpreters of *The Cherry Orchard* often position him as Chekhov's spokesman! But Chekhov undercuts the young revolutionary as much as he applauds him. For example, Trofimov reaches the apex of fine political rhetoric in an inappropriate setting. Consider his only love scene with Anya in Act II. He made his love for her clear to the audience at the end of Act I, but when he finally gets her alone, he launches into a fine political speech that includes his most frequently cited line, "All Russia is our orchard." His eloquence seems no more apropos than does Gayev's earlier pompous salute to a bookcase. Why does Trofimov not speak of his love? Anya responds with, "How well you speak!" Her words may be filled with awe, but they also draw attention to his speechifying. In Act III, Anya's mother accuses Trofimov of not yet understanding love. "You must become a man," she tells him, "at your age, you should understand those who love. And you yourself must love. . . ." She seems correct in her appraisal, as her accusation throws him literally off-balance. He exits, only to fall down the stairs, and this literal fall seems to be exactly what he needs. In Act IV, Trofimov says relatively little; instead, he forgives the teasing of others, looks for his galoshes, silently helps Anya

81. The translators of these options (in the order given in the text above) are Constance Garnet (*Four Great Plays by Anton Chekhov*. New York: Bantam Books, 1958); Ann Dunnigan (*Chekhov: The Major Plays*. New York: Signet, 1964); an anonymous translator (*Plays by Anton Chekhov*. New York: Concord Books, 1935); Carol Rocomora (*Chekhov: Four Plays*. Lyme: Smith and Kraus, 1996); David Mamet (*The Cherry Orchard by Anton Chekhov*. New York: Grove Press, 1985); Paul Schmidt (*The Plays of Anton Chekhov*. New York: Harper Perennial, 1999); and Michael Frayne (*Chekhov: Plays*. London: Methuen Drama, 1988). Ronald Hingley (*Five Major Plays by Anton Chekhov*. New York: Bantam Books, 1977) and Jean-Claude Van Itallie (*Chekhov: The Major Plays*. New York: Applause, 1995) also use "nincompoop."

pack, and finally ushers her into the future as they exit together. It seems that he has learned sympathy and the ability to express love through the ordinary actions of life.[82]

6. The Pause

Chekhov often calls for moments of silence in his plays by directing his characters to *pause* or by adding ellipses to their lines. In my translations I have scrupulously retained every devilish ". . ." that Chekhov uses in his Russian texts. Pauses and ellipses can suggest many different things: a thought that remains unspoken, the interruption of one character by another, a momentary lapse, confusion, embarrassment, or a willful refusal to speak. But whatever the function, during every pause or ellipsis something unspoken happens. As Nemirovich-Danchenko explains, "A pause is not something that is dead, but is an active intensification of experience."[83]

Consider Lopakhin's failure to propose to Varya in Act IV. Both their lines are punctuated by many ellipses, suggesting that they both speak haltingly. Their hesitant speech marks the tension between them. Chekhov also calls for three clear pauses in their scene. The first occurs soon after Varya enters, pretending to look for some lost item. When Lopakhin asks, "What are you looking for?" she keeps up the pretence: "I packed it myself and I can't remember where." Then, the first pause occurs. It is Lopakhin's turn to speak, but he delays. Is he so nervous that he does not know how to broach the subject of marriage? Or has he decided not to broach it at all? When he next speaks, he changes the subject: "Where are you going now, Varvara Mikhailovna?" After exhausting this topic and others concerning her future plans, Lopakhin next turns to the weather, as if proving the conventional wisdom that conversations about the weather always make for good small talk. He tells her that it's "three degrees below freezing," and she responds: "I didn't look. (*Pause.*) Besides, our thermometer is broken." What happens inside her head during this second pause? Does she compare the temperature of his love to the temperature outside? Is she wondering how she might raise the topic of marriage? Or is she merely at a loss for words? Lopakhin remains silent in a third "pause," perhaps the longest in the scene; it lasts until an offstage

82. See Bernard Beckerman, "Dramatic Analysis and Literary Interpretation: *The Cherry Orchard* as Exemplum," *New Literary History: A Journal of Thought and Interpretation* 2:3 (Spring 1971), 391–406.

83. Nemirovitch-Dantchenko [sic], *My Life in the Russian Theatre*, 163.

voice calls for him. Does Lopakhin think about marriage? Does he weigh Varya's positive and negative attributes? Or does he simply not know how to get out of the room? When he is finally called, Lopakhin "exits quickly." It is "as if he had been waiting for this call," Chekhov notes. This third pause ends both the scene and all hope for a proposal.

Although one cannot know for certain what happens in such moments of silence, one can infer much from the scene's context and the character's situation. Pauses create an illusion that Chekhov's characters are engaged in continuous thinking beyond what they actually say. Although words on a page are two-dimensional, the illusion that something lies underneath them has come to be known as the "subtext." Such moments challenge actors to decide why their characters stop speaking and to create the unspoken thoughts. The Moscow Art Theatre actors went on a "quest" to find the meanings behind each Chekhovian pause; they used "persistent and involved research, not merely external but also psychological."[84] This struggle led Stanislavsky to redefine the notion of a play. No longer could he view a dramatic text as a finished work of literary art; it became for him (and is for actors today) a blueprint from which to construct a finished performance by filling in the gaps with the artistry of acting.

7. The Music of Everyday Life

There is music of all sorts in Chekhov's plays, and *The Cherry Orchard* is no exception. Sometimes characters sing snatches of songs that reveal something of their attitudes toward life. In Act II Yasha and Yepikhodov croon a romantic ballad together as they both woo Dunyasha, and Lopakhin sings a satiric ditty about the power of wealth: "For money the Germans will turn the Russians into French."

Chekhov also uses background music in much the same way that melodrama does, to underscore the action in a scene. As Lyubov confesses her sins in Act II, a distant orchestra accompanies her words. Do the violins match or mock her sentimental story? In Act III, she hires the same orchestra for her inappropriately timed party. As her orchard is being auctioned off and she anxiously awaits news of its sale, the orchestra merrily plays a dissonant counterpoint to her emotional mood.

84. Ibid., 153.

Inspired by symbolism, Chekhov also makes his own music from the sounds of dialogue and daily life. His compositions are unique and startlingly beautiful, but easily missed in a quick read. Take another look at the moments in Act II that precede the Maeterlinckian sound of the snapping string, and you will find one of Chekhov's compositions. It begins when Yepikhodov walks across the stage playing a sad song on his guitar. Lyubov, "lost in thought," begins: "There's Yepikhodov . . ." Anya, also "lost in thought," joins the melody: "There's Yepikhodov . . ." Their absent-minded words say little, but repetition creates a meditative mood that seems to ebb and flow in the next few moments. Gayev picks up and embroiders the mood by beginning a hymn to nature, only to break it off when the others complain. The complaints strike a dissonant note, but this dissonance intensifies, rather than disrupts, the moody wave that engulfs the characters on stage. The mood builds to an apex when "everyone sits lost in thought." Their "silence" seems all the more magnified by "the quiet mumbling of Firs." This mumbling silence becomes the medium through which the otherworldly sound of the "snapping string" reverberates.

* * *

These seven items are intended only to whet your appetite for more. In my translation, I have been careful to reflect Chekhov (his semantics, repetitions, rhythms, grammar, ellipses, and so on) as closely as I could, so that you can find his devilish details on your own. Taste Chekhov's last play, and as you do, pay attention. The effort, I am certain, will pay rich rewards.

The Cherry Orchard

A Comedy in Four Acts

[When Chekhov wrote *The Cherry Orchard* in 1903, he was very ill; and yet, he considered his last play to be "not a drama at all, but a comedy; in places it's even a farce."[1] The Moscow Art Theatre premiered the play on what would be the author's last name-day, January 17, 1904. The production was directed by Konstantin Stanislavsky, who also played Gayev with wit. Olga Knipper played Lyubov Ranevskaya. The dramatic force of the production led the ill and consequently ill-tempered Chekhov to complain that Stanislavsky "ruined my play."[2] The English language premiere was in London in 1911; U.S. audiences saw the play first in Russian during the 1923 and 1924 Moscow Art Theatre tours and then in English in 1928. The translation that follows was created at the request of the Russian émigré director Lev Vainstein for a 1980 production at New York University's Tisch School of the Arts.[3] —SMC]

The Characters

Ranyévskaya, Lyubóv Andréyevna, a landowner. [Her first name means "love" in Russian. Her nickname is Lyúba. She is also called "Mámochka," a sweet form of "Mother," like "Mommy."]

Ánya, her daughter, seventeen years old. [Her nickname is Ánichka.]

Várya, Ranyevskaya's adopted daughter, twenty-four years old. [Varya is her nickname; her formal name is Varvára Mikháilovna.]

Gáyev, Léonid Andréyevich, Ranyevskaya's brother. [His nickname is Lyónya.]

Lopákhin, Yermoláy Alekséyevich, a merchant.

Trofímov, Pyótr Sergéyevich, a student. [His nickname is Pétya.]

Simeónov-Píshchik, Borís Borísovich, a landowner. [A *píshchik* is a sqeaking sound and a small whistle used to make the squeaking voice of a traditional Russian puppet.]

1. Chekhov to M. P. Lilina, September 15, 1903, in *Pis'ma* [Letters], vol. 11 (Moscow: Nauka, 1982), 248.

2. Chekhov to O. L. Knipper, March 29, 1904, in *Pis'ma* [Letters], vol. 12 (Moscow: Nauka, 1983), 74.

3. "[Carnicke's] *Cherry Orchard* is direct, easily accessible to young American students and mercifully free of all that blather that mucks up so much of the other versions that I know." James Parker, Professor of Theater, Virginia Commonwealth University, letter to the translator, May 8, 1986.

Charlótta Ivánovna, the governess. [Like Russian circus performers gener-
ally, her name is somewhat strange; she has a Germanic first name
and a Russian patronymic.]
Yepikhódov, Semyón Pantéléyevich, a clerk. [His name derives from the
Russian verb "to walk," suggesting that he is always underfoot.]
Dunyásha, the maid. [Her formal name is Avdótya Fyódorovna
Kozoyédova; her last name means "the goat-eater."]
Firs, a footman, an old man of eighty-seven. [He has an old-fashioned first
name; his formal name is Firs Nikoláyevich.]
Yásha, a young footman.
A passerby.
The station master.
A postal clerk.
Guests, servants.

The action takes place on the estate of L. A. Ranyevskaya.

Act I

A room which is still called the nursery. One door leads to
Anya's room. Dawn, the sun will soon rise. It is May; the cherries
are already in bloom, but in the garden it is cold; there is a
morning frost. The windows in the room are closed. Dunyasha
enters with a candle, and Lopakhin is holding a book.

LOPAKHIN: The train's arrived, thank God. What time is it?

DUNYASHA: Almost two. (*Puts out the candle.*) It's already light.

LOPAKHIN: How late was the train? Two hours at least. (*Yawns and
stretches.*) I'm a fine one, the devil I am! I come here especially
to meet them at the station and then oversleep . . . Dozed off
in the chair. Damn! . . . You could have woken me up.

DUNYASHA: I thought you left. (*Listens.*) Listen, I think they're
coming.

LOPAKHIN: (*Listens.*) No . . . They have to pick up the baggage
and all that . . . (*Pause.*) Lyubov Andreyevna lived abroad for
five years; I don't know what she's like now . . . She's a good
person. An easy-going simple person. I remember when I was
kid about fifteen, my late father—at that time he was a merchant, had a little store here in the country—he socked me in

the face and I got a bloody nose . . . We came here to the yard
for some reason and he was drunk too. I remember it like it
was yesterday. Lyubov Andreyevna—she was still so young, so
thin—she took me to the washstand, here in this very room, in
the nursery. "Don't cry, little peasant," she said, "you'll heal
before you marry . . ."[4] (*Pause.*) Little peasant . . . It's true, my
father was a peasant, but now I have a white waistcoat, and
yellow shoes. Still you can't make a silk purse out of a sow's
ear . . . I've made myself rich, got a lot of money but if you
think about it, sort it all out, a peasant's a peasant . . . (*Pages
through the book.*) You see, I've just read this book and didn't
understand a thing. I read and fell asleep.

Pause.

DUNYASHA: The dogs didn't sleep all night; they sense their masters
are coming.

LOPAKHIN: What's wrong with you, Dunyasha, you're so . . .

DUNYASHA: My hands are trembling. I'll faint.

LOPAKHIN: You're so very delicate, Dunyasha. And you dress like
a lady, even your hairdo. You musn't do that. You ought to
remember your place.

*Yepikhodov enters with a bouquet; he is dressed in
a jacket and in brightly polished boots that squeak
loudly; as he enters, he drops the bouquet.*

YEPIKHODOV: (*Picks up the bouquet.*) Here, the gardener sent these.
He says to put them in the dining room. (*Hands Dunyasha
the bouquet.*)

LOPAKHIN: And bring me some kvas.[5]

DUNYASHA: Yes, sir. (*Exits.*)

YEPIKHODOV: There's a morning frost now, three degrees below
freezing, but still the cherries are all in bloom. I cannot
approve of our climate. (*Sighs.*) I cannot. Our climate cannot
promote itself suitably. Look, Yermolay Alekseyevich, allow
me to add that I bought myself these boots three days ago,

4. A common expression of consolation.
5. A dark, nonalcoholic beer made from black bread.

and I dare to assure you, they squeak so much, it's impossible. What should I grease them with?

LOPAKHIN: Stop it. You bore me.

YEPIKHODOV: Everyday something bad happens to me. But I don't complain, I'm used to it, I even smile.

Dunyasha enters, hands Lopakhin a glass of kvas.

YEPIKHODOV: I'll go. (*Stumbles over a chair which falls.*) There . . . (*As if in triumph.*) There, you see, excuse the expression, but this kind of circumstance by the way . . . It's simply amazing! (*Exits.*)

DUNYASHA: I will tell you, Yermolay Alekseyevich, that Yepikhodov proposed to me!

LOPAKHIN: Ah!

DUNYASHA: I don't know how to . . . He's a quiet person, but sometimes, when he starts to talk, you don't understand anything. It's nice, and full of feeling, only incomprehensible. I sort of like him. He loves me madly. He's such an unlucky person, everyday there's something. We tease him about it too, call him "Twenty-Two Troubles" . . .

LOPAKHIN: (*Listens.*) Listen, I think they're coming . . .

DUNYASHA: They're coming! What's wrong with me . . . I'm so cold all over.

LOPAKHIN: They're actually coming. Let's go meet them. Will she recognize me? We haven't seen each other in five years.

DUNYASHA: (*Excited.*) I'll faint . . . Oh, I'll faint!

Two carriages are heard pulling up to the house. Lopakhin and Dunyasha quickly exit. The stage is empty. Noise begins in the neighboring rooms. Firs, leaning on a cane, hastily crosses the stage to meet Lyubov Andreyevna; he wears old-fashioned livery and a top hat; he mumbles something to himself, but it's impossible to make out a single word. The noise offstage gets louder and louder. A voice: "Let's go through here . . ." Lyubov Andreyevna, Anya, and Charlotta Ivanovna with a little dog on a chain, all of them dressed for traveling, enter; Varya enters wearing a coat and kerchief; Gayev, Simeonov-Pishchik, Lopakhin, Dunyasha carrying a bundle and an umbrella, and a servant with some bags all walk through the room.

ANYA: Let's go through here. Mama, remember what room this is?

LYUBOV ANDREYEVNA: (*Joyfully, through tears.*) The nursery!

VARYA: How cold it is! My hands feel numb. (*To Lyubov Andreyevna.*) Your rooms, the white room and the violet one, are just as you left them, Mamochka.

LYUBOV ANDREYEVNA: The nursery, my lovely beautiful room . . . I slept here when I was a baby . . . (*Cries.*) And now, I'm still like a baby . . . (*Kisses her brother, Varya, and then her brother again.*) Varya, you're just like you were before, you look like a nun. And I even recognize Dunyasha . . . (*Kisses Dunyasha.*)

GAYEV: The train was two hours late? How's that? How's that for management?

CHARLOTTA: (*To Pishchik.*) My dog eats nuts.

PISHCHIK: (*Surprised.*) Imagine that!

All exit except Anya and Dunyasha.

DUNYASHA: We waited up for you . . . (*Takes off Anya's coat and hat.*)

ANYA: I didn't sleep for four nights on the road . . . Now I'm frozen.

DUNYASHA: You left during Lent[6] and there was still snow on the ground, there was a frost, but now? My darling! (*Laughs and kisses Anya.*) I waited up for you, my joy, the light of my life . . . I'll tell you right now, I can't hold it back a minute longer . . .

ANYA: (*Languidly.*) Always something . . .

DUNYASHA: Just after Holy Week,[7] the clerk Yepikhodov proposed to me.

ANYA: You always talk about the same thing . . . (*Fixing her hair.*) I've lost all my hairpins . . . (*Very tired; even staggers.*)

DUNYASHA: Well I don't know what to think. He loves me, loves me so!

6. The forty-day period of fasting that precedes the resurrection of Christ on Easter Sunday, according to Christian tradition.

7. The seven-day period just before Easter, which includes Good Friday, when Christ was crucified.

ANYA: (*Glancing through the door to her room, gently.*) My room, my windows, as if I had never left. I'm home! Tomorrow morning I'll get up and run out into the orchard . . . Oh if only I could sleep! I didn't sleep the whole way, my worrying tired me out.

DUNYASHA: Three days ago Pyotr Sergeyevich got here.

ANYA: (*Joyously.*) Petya!

DUNYASHA: He's sleeping in the bathhouse, staying there too. "I'm afraid," he says, "to embarrass them." (*Looking at her pocket watch.*) I should wake him up, but Varvara Mikhailovna told me not to. "Don't wake him up," she said.

Varya enters, at her waist a ring of keys.

VARYA: Dunyasha, make some coffee, quick . . . Mamochka is asking for coffee.

DUNYASHA: Right away. (*Exits.*)

VARYA: Well thank God you're back. You're home again. (*Caressing her.*) Darling, you're back. My pretty one's back!

ANYA: I've been through so much.

VARYA: I can imagine!

ANYA: I got there during Holy Week. It was so cold then. Charlotta talked the whole way and kept doing her magic tricks. Why did you tie me down with Charlotta? . . .

VARYA: You couldn't go alone, dear. At seventeen!

ANYA: We got to Paris, it was cold, there was snow. I speak awful French. Mama was living on the fifth floor, and when I went to see her, she had some French ladies visiting her, and an old priest with a little book. It was smoky and uncomfortable. And suddenly I felt sorry for Mama, so sorry. I hugged her head, pressed her hands, and couldn't let go. Then she kept hugging me and crying . . .

VARYA: (*Through tears.*) Don't tell me, don't tell me . . .

ANYA: She'd already sold the summer house near Mentone.[8] She had nothing left, nothing. And I didn't have a kopeck left either. We almost didn't get back. But Mama didn't understand!

---

8. A town on the Mediterranean coast of France.

We sat down to eat at the station, and she ordered the most expensive thing, and tipped each waiter a ruble. Charlotta did the same. And Yasha ordered a full portion for himself, too. It was just awful. You know Yasha is Mama's footman now. We brought him back with us too . . .

VARYA: I saw the scoundrel.

ANYA: Well, how are things going? Did you pay the interest?

VARYA: With what.

ANYA: My God, my God . . .

VARYA: In August the estate will be sold . . .

ANYA: My God . . .

LOPAKHIN: (*Looks in at the door and moos.*) Moo-oo . . . (*Exits.*)

VARYA: (*Through tears.*) If only I could give it to him . . . (*Threatens with a fist.*)

ANYA: (*Embraces Varya, softly.*) Varya, did he propose to you? (*Varya shakes her head no.*) But I'm sure he loves you . . . Why don't you talk it over with each other? What are you waiting for?

VARYA: I just think nothing will come of it. He's always busy; he has no time for me . . . He pays no attention. So to hell with him! It's hard for me seeing him . . . Everybody talks about our wedding, everybody congratulates me, but actually there's nothing there; it's all like a dream . . . (*In another tone of voice.*) You have a brooch like a bee.

ANYA: (*Sadly.*) Mama bought it. (*Goes toward her room, talking gaily like a child.*) And I flew over Paris in a big balloon.

VARYA: My dear one's back, you're back! My pretty one's back!

Dunyasha has entered with the coffee pot and makes coffee.

VARYA: (*Standing near the door.*) I fuss with the housework, dear, all day long, but still I dream. If only we could marry you to a rich man, then I'd feel calm. I would go to the local hermitage,[9] then to Kiev . . . To Moscow. And I would walk from holy place to holy place . . . Just walk and walk. How splendid!

9. A secluded retreat for a holy person, similar to a monastery or convent.

ANYA: The birds are singing in the orchard. What time is it now?

VARYA: It must be close to three. You should go to sleep, darling. (*Leads Anya into her room and exits.*) How splendid!

Yasha enters with a lap robe and a traveling case.

YASHA: (*Crosses the stage, daintily.*) Can one walk through here, *mademoiselle?*

DUNYASHA: I didn't recognize you, Yasha. How you've changed while you were abroad!

YASHA: Hmmm . . . And who are you?

DUNYASHA: When you left, I was still . . . (*Measures her height from the floor.*) Dunyasha, Fyódor Kozoyédov's daughter. You don't remember!

YASHA: Hmmm . . . a juicy little cucumber! (*Glances around and then embraces her; she cries out and drops a saucer. Yasha quickly exits.*)

VARYA: (*At the door, annoyed.*) What's happening here?

DUNYASHA: (*Through tears.*) I broke a saucer . . .

VARYA: That's a good sign.

ANYA: (*Coming out of her room.*) We should warn Mama that Petya's here . . .

VARYA: I told them not to wake him up.

ANYA: (*Meditatively.*) Six years ago Father died, a month later, our brother Grísha drowned in the river, a cute little seven-year-old boy. Mama couldn't bear it, and left, left without looking back . . . (*Sighs.*) How I understand her, if only she knew! (*Pause.*) And Petya Trofimov was Grisha's teacher, he might remind her . . .

Enter Firs; he wears a jacket and a white waistcoat.

FIRS: (*Goes to the coffee-maker, fussily.*) The mistress will have a bite to eat in here . . . (*Puts on white gloves.*) Is the coffee ready? (*Sternly to Dunyasha.*) You! Where's the cream?

DUNYASHA: Oh, my God . . . (*Exits quickly.*)

FIRS: (*Fusses over the coffee-maker.*) Ugh, you nincompoop . . . (*Mumbles to himself.*) She's come back from Paris. The master went to Paris once . . . by horse . . . (*Laughs.*)

VARYA: What's that, Firs?

FIRS: What is it you wish? (*Joyfully.*) My lady has come back! I waited up! Now I can die . . . (*Cries with joy.*)

Enter Lyubov Andreyevna, Gayev, and Simeonov-Pishchik. Pishchik wears a long pleated Russian coat, made from soft material, and loose Turkish trousers. Gayev motions with his hands and his body as if he were playing billiards.

LYUBOV ANDREYEVNA: How does it go? Let me remember . . . Yellow ball off the side! A rebound to the center!

GAYEV: Cut to the center![10] Once, you and I, sister, slept in this very room and now I'm fifty-one years old, strange as it may seem . . .

LOPAKHIN: Yes, time flies.

GAYEV: How's that?

LOPAKHIN: Time, I say, flies.

GAYEV: It smells of patchouli[11] here.

ANYA: I'm going to sleep. Good night, Mama. (*Kisses her mother.*)

LYUBOV ANDREYEVNA: My beloved child. (*Kisses Anya's hands.*) Are you glad to be home? I can't seem to collect myself.

ANYA: Goodnight, Uncle.

GAYEV: (*Kisses Anya's face and hands.*) God be with you. How much you look like your mother! (*To his sister.*) Lyuba, at her age, you looked exactly like this.

---

10. Addicted to the game of billiards, Gayev uses its jargon throughout the play. He plays a version called carom billiards with three balls; wooden cue sticks manipulate the balls on a cloth-covered table with raised and cushioned sides. More familiar in the United States is the version called pocket billiards (or pool). Significantly, billiards uses indirection and angles to hit balls around the table, a kind of action that mirrors the oblique and often passive-aggressive interaction among Chekhov's characters.

11. A powerfully aromatic oil made from an East Indian plant.

Anya gives her hand to Lopakhin and to Pishchik;
exits, closing the door behind her.

LYUBOV ANDREYEVNA: She's very tired.

PISHCHIK: The road, of course, was long.

VARYA: (*To Lopakhin and Pishchik.*) Well, gentlemen? It's nearly
three, time to pay your respects.

LYUBOV ANDREYEVNA: (*Laughs.*) You're still the same, Varya.
(*Draws Varya toward herself, and kisses her.*) I'll drink my
coffee, then we'll all go. (*Firs puts a pillow under her feet.*)
Thank you. You're like family. I've gotten used to coffee. I
drink it day and night. Thank you, my sweet old man. (*Kisses
Firs.*)

VARYA: I'll look to see if they brought in all the things . . . (*Exits.*)

LYUBOV ANDREYEVNA: Is it really me sitting here? (*Laughs.*) I feel
like jumping, waving my arms. (*Covers her face with her
hands.*) But what if I'm only asleep! God can see I love my
homeland, love it tenderly, I couldn't look out of the train,
cried the whole way. (*Through tears.*) However, I must drink
my coffee. Thank you, Firs, thank you, my sweet old man. I'm
so glad that you're still alive.

FIRS: Day before yesterday.

GAYEV: He's hard of hearing.

LOPAKHIN: I have to go now, at five o'clock in the morning I have
to leave for Khárkov.[12] Damn it! I wanted to look at you, talk
to you . . . You're still such a splendid woman . . .

PISHCHIK: (*Breathing heavily.*) Even more beautiful . . . Dressed
in the Parisian fashion . . . Can't help falling for you, come
what may . . .

LOPAKHIN: Your brother here, Leonid Andreyevich, says that I am
a boor and a peasant, but it's all the same to me. Let him
say what he wants. I only want you to trust me as you did
before, to look at me with your surprising, touching eyes as
before. God have mercy! My father was your father's and

---

12. An important cultural and mercantile center in the northeastern part of
the Ukraine, with a university that dates from 1805; railroad transportation
made it a hub for trade.

grandfather's serf, but you, particularly you, have done so much for me that I can forget all that. I love you like my own family . . . More than my family.

LYUBOV ANDREYEVNA: I can't sit still, I'm in no condition . . . (*Jumps up and walks about in high agitation.*) I won't survive this joy . . . Laugh at me, I'm stupid . . . My own dear cupboard . . . (*Kisses the cupboard.*) My little table . . .

GAYEV: While you were away, the nurse died.

LYUBOV ANDREYEVNA: (*Sits down and drinks coffee.*) Yes, God rest her soul. They wrote me.

GAYEV: And Anastásia died. Petrúshka,[13] the cross-eyed one, left me and went to live in town with the police officer. (*Takes a box of fruit-drops out of his pocket, sucks on one.*)

PISHCHIK: My daughter Dáshenka . . . sends you her regards . . .

LOPAKHIN: I want to tell you something pleasant, happy. (*Looks at his watch.*) I'm going now. I don't have time to chat . . . Well, so, I'll just say two or three words. You already know that the cherry orchard is to be sold to pay your debts. The auction is set for August 22nd. But don't worry, my dear one, sleep easy, there is a way out . . . Here is my plan. Pay attention now! Your estate is located only thirteen miles from town, and the railroad runs close by, so if the cherry orchard and the land near the river were cleared for small plots and leased for summer houses, then you would have at the least twenty-five thousand rubles a year income.

GAYEV: Excuse me, but that's nonsense!

LYUBOV ANDREYEVNA: I don't quite understand you, Yermolay Alekseyevich.

LOPAKHIN: You could get at the least twenty-five rubles a year for every two-and-a-half-acre plot, and if you advertise now, I guarantee you that by autumn you won't have one free scrap of land, everything will be snapped up. In short, congratulations, you are saved. The site is wonderful, the river is deep. But you'll have to tidy it up, of course, clear the land . . . For example, you'll have to take down the old structures, like this

---

13. The nickname for Pyotr and a popular Russian puppet that uses the *pishchik* whistle as its voice.

house, which isn't really needed now, and cut down the old cherry orchard . . .

LYUBOV ANDREYEVNA: Cut it down? Darling, forgive me, but you don't understand at all. If there's anything in the county you can point to as interesting, even remarkable, it can only be our cherry orchard.

LOPAKHIN: The only remarkable thing about this orchard is that it is very big. You get cherries only once every two years and then you can't get rid of them, nobody buys them.

GAYEV: But this orchard is so remarkable, it's even mentioned in the encyclopedia.

LOPAKHIN: (*Looking at his watch.*) If we don't think of anything or come to any conclusion, then on August 22nd, both the cherry orchard and the whole estate will be sold at auction. Make up your minds! There's no other way out, I swear to you. None, none.

FIRS: In the old days, about forty or fifty years ago, they dried the cherries, soaked them, marinated them, boiled them into jam, and they used to . . .

GAYEV: Be quiet, Firs.

FIRS: And they used to send off cartloads of dried cherries to Moscow, and to Kharkov. There was money then! And the dried cherries were so soft, juicy, sweet, fragrant . . . They knew the way to do it . . .

LYUBOV ANDREYEVNA: And where is the "way to do it" now?

FIRS: Forgotten. No one remembers.

PISHCHIK: (*To Lyubov Andreyevna.*) What's it like in Paris? How is it? Did you eat frogs?

LYUBOV ANDREYEVNA: I ate crocodiles.

PISHCHIK: Imagine that . . .

LOPAKHIN: Until now there were only masters and peasants in the country, but now these summer folk have appeared. All the cities, even the smallest ones, are surrounded by summer houses now. And it's safe to say that in twenty-five years the summer folk will multiply surprisingly fast. Now they only drink tea on their porches, but maybe they will take to cultivating their acres, and then your cherry orchard will be happy, rich, luxuriant . . .

GAYEV: (*Annoyed.*) What nonsense!

Enter Varya and Yasha.

VARYA: Here, Mamochka, there are two telegrams for you. (*Chooses a key and with a jingle opens an old-fashioned cupboard.*) Here they are.

LYUBOV ANDREYEVNA: From Paris. (*Tears them up without reading them.*) I'm finished with Paris . . .

GAYEV: Do you know, Lyuba, how old this cupboard is? A week ago I took out the bottom drawer, looked at it, and saw a date burned into it. This cupboard was made exactly one hundred years ago. How's that? Ah? Maybe we should celebrate its centennial. An inanimate object, but still, however you look at it, a cupboard for books.

PISHCHIK: (*Surprised.*) A hundred years . . . Imagine that! . . .

GAYEV: Yes . . . Quite something . . . (*Feeling the cupboard.*) Dear respected cupboard! I salute your existence, which has been directed for over one hundred years toward the glorious ideals of goodness and justice. Your silent appeal to fruitful labor has not weakened during the course of one hundred years, sustaining courage (*Through tears.*) and faith in a better future through generations of our family and engendering in us ideals of goodness and social consciousness.

Pause.

LOPAKHIN: Yes . . .

LYUBOV ANDREYEVNA: You're still the same, Lyonya.

GAYEV: (*A little confused.*) Straight to the right corner! Cut to the center! . . .

LOPAKHIN: (*Looking at his watch.*) Well, it's time for me to go.

YASHA: (*Hands Lyubov Andreyevna her medicine.*) Perhaps you should take your pills now.

PISHCHIK: You shouldn't take medications, darling one . . . Does no good, does no harm . . . Give it here, please . . . Madam. (*Takes the pills, blows on them, places them in his mouth, then washes them down with kvas.*) There!

LYUBOV ANDREYEVNA: (*Frightened.*) You've gone mad!

PISHCHIK: I took all the pills.

LOPAKHIN: What a glutton! (*All laugh.*)

FIRS: His excellency came to see us during Holy Week and ate half a bucket of our cucumbers . . . (*Mumbles.*)

LYUBOV ANDREYEVNA: What is he talking about?

VARYA: He's been mumbling for three years now. We're used to it.

YASHA: Senility.

Charlotta Ivanovna, in a white dress, very thin, straight-laced, with a lorgnette hanging at her waist, crosses the stage.

LOPAKHIN: Forgive me, Charlotta Ivanovna, I haven't had the chance to say hello to you. (*Tries to kiss her hand.*)

CHARLOTTA: (*Pulling her hand away.*) If I allow you to kiss my hand, then you'll want to kiss my elbow, then my shoulder . . .

LOPAKHIN: It's not my day today. (*All laugh.*) Charlotta Ivanovna, show us a trick!

LYUBOV ANDREYEVNA: Charlotta, show us a trick!

CHARLOTTA: Not now. I want to go to sleep. (*Exits.*)

LOPAKHIN: In three weeks we'll see each other again. (*Kisses Lyubov Andreyevna's hand.*) Goodbye for now. It's time to go. (*To Gayev.*) Goodbye. (*Exchanges kisses on the cheeks with Pishchik.*) Goodbye. (*Gives his hand to Varya, then to Firs and to Yasha.*) I don't want to leave. (*To Lyubov Andreyevna.*) If you think about the summer houses and decide to do it, then let me know, and I'll get you a loan of fifty thousand. Think it over seriously.

VARYA: (*Angrily.*) Go, if you're going!

LOPAKHIN: I'm going, I'm going . . . (*Goes.*)

GAYEV: Boor! Well, *pardon* . . . Varya's going to marry him. He's Varya's *beau*.[14]

VARYA: Don't talk, Uncle, about unnecessary things.

---

14. "Pardon me"; "boyfriend" (French).

LYUBOV ANDREYEVNA: What's wrong, Varya? I would be happy for you. He's a good person.

PISHCHIK: A person, to tell the truth . . . most worthy . . . and my Dashenka also says that . . . She says various things. (*Snores, but immediately wakes up.*) But all the same, madam, allow me . . . a loan of two hundred and forty rubles . . . Tomorrow I must pay the interest on my mortgage . . .

VARYA: (*Frightened.*) We've nothing, nothing!

LYUBOV ANDREYEVNA: I really do have nothing.

PISHCHIK: It'll turn up! (*Laughs.*) I never lose hope. You see, just when I thought everything was lost, ruined, then lo and behold, the railroad went through my land and . . . They paid me for it. And then, too, something else might happen, if not today, tomorrow . . . Maybe Dashenka will win two hundred thousand . . . She has a lottery ticket.

LYUBOV ANDREYEVNA: The coffee's drunk, now we can go to bed.

FIRS: (*Brushes off Gayev's clothes and scolds.*) You put on the wrong trousers again. What am I going to do with you?

VARYA: (*Softly.*) Anya's asleep. (*Quietly opens the window.*) The sun's up already, it's not cold. Look, Mamochka, what wonderful trees! My God, the air! The starlings are singing!

GAYEV: (*Opens the other window.*) The orchard is all white. You didn't forget, Lyuba? There's that long avenue of trees that lies so straight, just like a taut belt. It shines on moonlit nights. Do you remember? You didn't forget?

LYUBOV ANDREYEVNA: (*Looks out the window into the orchard.*) Oh my childhood, my purity! I slept in this nursery, looked from here out into the orchard, happiness awoke with me every morning, and the orchard was just the same then, nothing has changed! (*Laughs from joy.*) All, all white! Oh my orchard! After a dark rainy autumn and a cold winter, you're still young, full of happiness. Heavenly angels have not deserted you . . . If I could take this heavy stone off my chest, and off my shoulders, if I could forget my past!

GAYEV: Yes, and the orchard will be sold to pay the debts, strange as it may seem . . .

LYUBOV ANDREYEVNA: Look, our late mama is walking in the orchard . . . in a white dress! (*Laughs from joy.*) It's her!

GAYEV: Where?

VARYA: God be with you, Mamochka!

LYUBOV ANDREYEVNA: No one's there, I imagined it. On the right, as the path turns toward the gazebo, there's a little white tree that's bent over, it looks like a woman . . .

Trofimov enters in a shabby student uniform and glasses.

LYUBOV ANDREYEVNA: What an amazing orchard! Masses of white flowers, blue sky . . .

TROFIMOV: Lyubov Andreyevna! (*She looks around at him.*) I only want to pay my respects and then I'll leave. (*Kisses her hand warmly.*) I was told to wait until morning, but I didn't have enough patience.

Lyubov Andreyevna looks at him, confused.

VARYA: (*Through tears.*) This is Petya Trofimov . . .

TROFIMOV: Petya Trofimov, Grisha's former teacher . . . Have I changed so much?

Lyubov Andreyevna embraces him, and quietly cries.

GAYEV: (*Embarrassed.*) Enough, enough, Lyuba.

VARYA: (*Cries.*) I told you, Petya, that it could wait until tomorrow.

LYUBOV ANDREYEVNA: My Grisha . . . my little boy . . . Grisha . . . my son . . .

VARYA: What can we do, Mamochka. It's God's will.

TROFIMOV: (*Softly, through tears.*) Don't, don't . . .

LYUBOV ANDREYEVNA: (*Quietly cries.*) My little boy died, drowned . . . For what? For what, my friend? (*More quietly.*) Anya's asleep in the next room, and I'm talking so loudly . . . Making noise . . . What's the matter, Petya? Why have you lost your looks? Why have you gotten so old?

TROFIMOV: In the train an old woman called me a "shabby lord."

LYUBOV ANDREYEVNA: You were such a young boy then, a good-looking student, and now your hair is thin, glasses. Are you really still a student? (*Goes toward the door.*)

TROFIMOV: I'll probably be an eternal student.[15]

LYUBOV ANDREYEVNA: (*Kisses her brother, then Varya.*) Well, let's go to sleep. You've gotten old too, Leonid.

PISHCHIK: (*Following her.*) That means it's time to sleep now . . . Oh, my gout.[16] I'll stay here for the night . . . Perhaps then, Lyubov Andreyevna, dear heart, tomorrow morning, bright and early . . . Two hundred and forty rubles . . .

GAYEV: Always talking about his own problems.

PISHCHIK: Two hundred and forty rubles . . . have to pay the interest on my mortgage.

LYUBOV ANDREYEVNA: I don't have any money, dear friend.

PISHCHIK: I'll give it back, darling . . . a trivial sum . . .

LYUBOV ANDREYEVNA: Well, all right, Leonid will give it to you . . . Give it to him, Leonid.

GAYEV: I'll give it to him all right!

LYUBOV ANDREYEVNA: What's to be done, give it . . . He needs it . . . He'll give it back.

Lyubov Andreyevna, Trofimov, Pishchik, and Firs exit. Gayev, Varya, and Yasha are left on stage.

GAYEV: My sister is not yet unused to squandering her money. (*To Yasha.*) Go away, lad, you smell like a henhouse.

YASHA: (*With a smirk.*) And you, Leonid Andreyevich, are just like you were.

GAYEV: How's that? (*To Varya.*) What did he say?

VARYA: (*To Yasha.*) Your mother's come from the country. She's been sitting in the servants' quarters since yesterday. She wants to see you . . .

---

15. Students with radical political leanings and liberal social ideas, such as Trofimov, were often suspended or expelled from schools by the tsarist government; they could even be exiled from the country.

16. A disease characterized by swelling of the joints in the legs.

YASHA: To hell with her!

VARYA: Ah, you should be ashamed!

YASHA: She's all I need now! She could have come tomorrow. (*Exits.*)

VARYA: Mamochka is the same as she ever was, hasn't changed a bit. If she had her way, she'd give everything away.

GAYEV: Yes . . . (*Pause.*) If they prescribe a lot of remedies for some sickness or other, it means that the sickness is incurable. I think, I strain my brain, I come up with a lot of remedies, a lot, but that means, in fact, that I don't have one. It would be good to receive an inheritance from someone, good to marry Anya to a very rich man, good to go to Yaroslávl and try our luck with our aunt the Countess.[17] Our aunt is very rich, after all. Very rich.

VARYA: (*Cries.*) If only God would help us.

GAYEV: Don't whine. Our aunt is rich, but she doesn't like us. In the first place, my sister married a lawyer, not a nobleman . . .

Anya appears at the doorway.

GAYEV: Didn't marry a nobleman, and you can't say that she exactly conducts herself virtuously . . . She's a fine, good, wonderful woman, I love her very much, but, however you allow for extenuating circumstances, you still have to admit that she's wanton. You can feel it in her every move.

VARYA: (*In a whisper.*) Anya's standing at the door.

GAYEV: How's that? (*Pause.*) That's odd. Something's gotten into my right eye . . . I'm not seeing well. And Thursday, when I was at the district court . . .

Anya enters.

VARYA: Why aren't you asleep, Anya?

ANYA: I can't fall asleep. I can't.

---

17. A city on the upper Volga River, founded in medieval times; it once served as Russia's capital. The fact that their aunt is a countess underlines the family's connection to Russia's royalty.

GAYEV: My little sweet. (*Kisses Anya's face, her hands.*) My child . . . (*Through tears.*) You're not my niece, you're my angel, you're everything to me. Trust me, trust me . . .

ANYA: I trust you, Uncle. We all love you, respect you . . . but my darling uncle, you should keep quiet, just keep quiet. What did you just say about my Mama, about your own sister? Why did you say that?

GAYEV: Yes, yes . . . (*Covers his face with his hands.*) It really is awful! My God! God, save me! And today I made a speech to the cupboard . . . So stupid! And only when I finished did I understand how stupid!

VARYA: It's true, Uncle, you should keep quiet. Just keep quiet.

ANYA: If you'll keep quiet, then even you will feel calmer.

GAYEV: I'll keep quiet. (*Kisses Anya's hands and Varya's hands.*) I'll keep quiet. But one thing about business. Thursday, I was at the district court, and well, a group gathered, we started to talk about this and that, one thing and another, and it seems that maybe I could arrange a loan on a promissory note in order to pay the interest at the bank.

VARYA: If only God would help!

GAYEV: Tuesday, I'll go and talk about it again. (*To Varya.*) Don't whine. (*To Anya.*) Your mama will talk to Lopakhin. He, of course, won't refuse her . . . And you, when you're rested, you'll go to Yaroslavl to your great aunt, the Countess. So that's what we'll do, from three sides—and it's in the bag! We'll pay the interest, I'm sure of it . . . (*Puts a candy in his mouth.*) On my honor, I'll swear by whatever you like, the estate won't be sold! (*Excitedly.*) I'll swear by my own happiness. Here's my hand. Call me a worthless, dishonorable man if I allow the auction to take place. By my whole being, I swear!

ANYA: (*A calm mood returns to her; she is happy.*) How good you are, Uncle, how smart! (*Hugs her uncle.*) I'm calm now! I'm calm! I'm happy.

Firs enters.

FIRS: (*Reproachfully.*) Leonid Andreyevich, don't you fear God! When will you go to sleep?

GAYEV: Right away, right away. You go along, Firs. It's all right, I'll undress myself. Well, children, lullaby and goodnight . . . The details tomorrow, and now, it's time to go to sleep. (*Kisses Anya and Varya.*) I'm a man of the eighties[18] . . . They don't value that decade much these days, and I can say that I have indeed suffered for my convictions during my life. Not for nothing does the peasant love me. A peasant should know! Should know what kind of . . .

ANYA: You're at it again, Uncle!

VARYA: Keep quiet, Uncle dear.

FIRS: (*Angrily.*) Leonid Andreyevich!

GAYEV: Coming, coming . . . Go to sleep! Off both sides to the center! I'll sink the white ball . . . (*Exits with Firs hobbling after him.*)

ANYA: Now I'm calm. I don't feel like going to Yaroslavl. I don't like my great aunt, but still I'm calm. Thanks to Uncle. (*Sits.*)

VARYA: You must sleep. I'll go. Oh, while you were away, something unpleasant happened here. In the old servants' quarters, you know, where only the old servants live, Yefímushka, Pólya, Yevstignéy,[19] and Karp too. They started letting all kinds of good-for-nothings spend the night—and I kept quiet. But then I heard a rumor that I ordered them to be fed only peas. From stinginess, you understand . . . And it's all Yevstigney's fault . . . All right, I thought. If they think that, just you wait. So I called for Yevstigney. (*Yawns.*) He came . . . "How is it" I say to Yevstigney . . . "that you're such a fool . . ." (*Looking at Anya.*) Anichka! . . . (*Pause.*) She's asleep . . . (*Takes Anya by the arm.*) Let's put you to bed. Let's go . . . (*Leads Anya.*) My darling is asleep! Let's go. (*They go.*)

Far beyond the orchard a shepherd plays on a pipe. Trofimov crosses the stage, and, upon seeing Varya and Anya, stops.

VARYA: Shh . . . She's asleep . . . asleep . . . Let's go, my own.

---

18. During the 1880s under the repressive reign of Alexander III, Russia's social reformers were unable to effect any significant changes; they could only improve living conditions among peasants in small, localized ways.

19. An old-fashioned name.

ANYA: (*Softly, half asleep.*) I'm so tired . . . Everywhere little bells . . . Uncle . . . dear, and Mama and Uncle . . .

VARYA: Let's go, my own, let's go . . . (*They go into Anya's room.*)

TROFIMOV: (*Tenderly.*) My sunlight! My spring!

Curtain.

Act II

A field. An old, lopsided, long-neglected chapel; near it a well. Big stones that apparently once were gravestones, and an old bench. The road to Gayev's manor house can be seen. On one side, poplars loom up darkly; that is where the cherry orchard begins. In the distance, a row of telegraph poles, and far, far away, on the horizon one can barely make out a big city, that can only be seen well in good, clear weather. Soon the sun will set. Charlotta, Yasha, and Dunyasha are sitting on the bench; Yepikhodov stands nearby and plays something sad on a guitar; all sit lost in thought. Charlotta wears an old peaked cap; she takes a gun from her shoulder and fixes the buckle on the strap.

CHARLOTTA: (*Deep in thought.*) I don't have a real passport, I don't know how old I am, but I think I'm quite young. When I was a little girl, my father and Mama went around to the fairs[20] and gave performances, very good ones. And I jumped the *salto mortale*[21] and did various tricks. And when Papa and Mama died, a certain German lady took me in and began to educate me. It was good. I grew up, then became a governess. But where I came from and who I am—I don't know . . . Who my parents were, whether they were even married . . . I don't know . . . (*Takes a cucumber out of her pocket and eats.*) I don't know anything. (*Pause.*) I feel so much like talking to someone . . . I don't have anyone.

YEPIKHODOV: (*Plays the guitar and sings.*) "What care I for the din of the world. What are friends or foes to me . . ."[22] How pleasant it is to play the mandolin!

20. Russian annual fairs featured puppet shows, dancing bears, circus acts, and theatrical presentations.
21. "Leap of death" (Italian).
22. A soulful ballad.

DUNYASHA: That's a guitar, not a mandolin. (*Looks in a pocket mirror and powders her nose.*)

YEPIKHODOV: For a man mad with love, this is a mandolin. (*Continuing the song.*) "If only my heart could be set aglow (*Yasha sings along.*) by requited love from thee!"

CHARLOTTA: These people sing so badly . . . Ugh! Like jackals.

DUNYASHA: (*To Yasha.*) But still, what happiness to have gone abroad!

YASHA: Yes, of course. I can't help but agree with you. (*Yawns and lights a cigar.*)

YEPIKHODOV: An understandable point. Abroad, everything long ago reached its full development.

YASHA: That goes without saying!

YEPIKHODOV: I am a well-developed person, I read various marvelous books, but somehow I can't understand the direction in which I personally feel like going, to live or to shoot myself, personally speaking. But just in case, I always carry a revolver on me. Here it is . . . (*Shows the revolver.*)

CHARLOTTA: I'm finished. Now I'm going. (*Puts the gun over her shoulder.*) You, Yepikhodov, are a very intelligent person and very frightening. Women must love you madly. Brrr! (*Goes.*) All these smart ones are still so stupid. There's no one for me to talk to . . . Always alone. Alone, I have no one and . . . And who I am, why I am, remains unknown . . . (*Exits slowly.*)

YEPIKHODOV: Personally speaking, not referring to other objects, I must express myself, by the way, on the subject that fate treats me without compassion, like a storm treats a small ship. If, let's say, I am mistaken, then why should I wake up this morning, let's take this as an example, I wake up, look down, and on my chest there's a frightening, gigantic spider . . . like that. (*Measures it with both hands.*) Or also, I take some kvas to drink, and look, there in the bottom of the glass is something most improper, something like a cockroach. (*Pause.*) Have you read the English historian, Buckle?[23] (*Pause.*) I would like, Avdotya Fyodorovna, to bother you a little with a word or two.

23. Henry Thomas Buckle (1821–1862), author of *History of Civilization* (1861), was popular among liberal thinkers in Russia.

DUNYASHA: Speak.

YEPIKHODOV: But I would like to speak with you in private . . . (*Sighs.*)

DUNYASHA: (*Embarrassed.*) All right . . . Only first bring me my wrap. It's near the cupboard . . . It's a little damp out here . . .

YEPIKHODOV: Yes, madam . . . I'll bring it, madam . . . Now I know what to do with my revolver . . . (*Takes the guitar and plays as he exits.*)

YASHA: Twenty-Two Troubles! A stupid person, just between us. (*Yawns.*)

DUNYASHA: God forbid he shoot himself! (*Pause.*) I've become so excitable, everything upsets me. When I was still a little girl, they brought me to live with the masters and now I'm unused to the simple life. Just look how softest-soft my hands are, like a lady's. I've become so tender, so delicate, well-bred, I'm afraid of everything . . . Frighteningly so. And Yasha, if you were to deceive me, I don't know what would happen to my nerves.

YASHA: (*Kisses her.*) My juicy little cucumber! Of course, every girl should rein herself in. What I dislike more than anything else, is a girl who behaves improperly.

DUNYASHA: I've fallen passionately in love with you, you're so educated, you can discuss everything. (*Pause.*)

YASHA: Yes, madam . . . In my opinion, it's like this: if a girl loves someone, then that means she's immoral. (*Pause.*) It's pleasant smoking cigars out in the fresh air . . . (*Listens.*) Someone's coming this way . . . It's the masters . . .

Dunyasha impulsively hugs him.

YASHA: Go home, as if you had gone for a swim in the river, go by that path there, or else they'll meet you and think that I was out here with you. I can't stand this.

DUNYASHA: (*Softly coughs.*) My head's spinning from your cigars. (*Exits.*)

Yasha remains; he sits down near the chapel. Enter Lyubov Andreyevna, Gayev, and Lopakhin.

LOPAKHIN: You must decide once and for all. Time will not wait for you. There's no point in questioning it. Do you agree to rent your land for summer houses or not? Answer in one word. Yes or no? Only one word!

LYUBOV ANDREYEVNA: Who's been smoking those revolting cigars here . . . (*Sits down.*)

GAYEV: Once they built the railroad, it became so convenient. (*Sits down.*) We ride into town and have lunch . . . Green ball to the center! I'd like to go home first, and play a game.

LYUBOV ANDREYEVNA: You'll have time later.

LOPAKHIN: Only one word! (*Pleadingly.*) Give me your answer!

GAYEV: (*Yawning.*) How's that?

LYUBOV ANDREYEVNA: (*Looks in her purse.*) Yesterday there was a lot of money, but today there's so little. My poor Varya feeds everybody milk soup to economize, and in the kitchen they eat only peas, but I waste money senselessly . . . (*Drops her purse and her gold pieces scatter.*) There, they're strewn all over the place . . . (*Annoyed.*)

YASHA: Allow me, I'll get them. (*Collects the change.*)[24]

LYUBOV ANDREYEVNA: If you'd be so kind, Yasha. Why did I go out to lunch anyway . . . Your restaurant is wretched, with its music and tablecloths that smell of soap . . . Why do you drink so much, Lyonya? Why do you eat so much? Why do you talk so much? Today in the restaurant you talked a lot again, and none of it was to the point. About the seventies, about the decadents![25] And to whom? You talk to the waiters about the decadents!

LOPAKHIN: Yes.

GAYEV: (*Waves his hands.*) I'm incorrigible, that's obvious . . . (*Annoyed by Yasha.*) What's this, why are you always twirling about in front of me?

YASHA: (*Laughs.*) I can't help laughing when I hear your voice.

---

24. Following the Moscow Art Theatre's staging of this moment, actors playing Yasha often pocket coins as they collect them.

25. During the 1870s, before the reign of Alexander III, reformers known as Populists initiated major social changes in the education of the peasantry. Symbolist writers were derogatorily called decadents.

GAYEV: (*To his sister.*) It's either him or me . . .

LYUBOV ANDREYEVNA: Go away, Yasha, run along . . .

YASHA: (*Gives Lyubov Andreyevna her purse.*) Now I'll go. (*Hardly keeps from laughing.*) This minute . . . (*Exits.*)

LOPAKHIN: The rich Derigánov plans to buy your estate. He's going himself, personally, they say, to the sale.

LYUBOV ANDREYEVNA: And where did you hear that?

LOPAKHIN: They're talking about it in town.

GAYEV: Our aunt from Yaroslavl promised to send something, but when and how much we don't know . . .

LOPAKHIN: How much will she send? One hundred thousand? Two hundred thousand?

LYUBOV ANDREYEVNA: Well . . . Ten thousand . . . or fifteen, and for that we'll be grateful.

LOPAKHIN: Excuse me, I've never met such frivolous people as you, such unbusiness-like, strange people. I'm telling you plainly that your estate will be sold, and you simply don't understand.

LYUBOV ANDREYEVNA: What can we do? Teach us what?

LOPAKHIN: I teach you every day. Every day I tell you one and the same thing . . . Both the cherry orchard and the land by the river must be rented for summer houses. Do that now, immediately, the auction is on top of you! Understand? Once you decide, once and for all, that there should be summer houses, then you'll get all the money you need, and then you'll be saved.

LYUBOV ANDREYEVNA: Summer houses and summer folk—it's so vulgar, forgive me.

GAYEV: I completely agree with you.

LOPAKHIN: I'll either sob, or I'll yell, or I'll faint. I can't stand it! You're torturing me! (*To Gayev.*) You're an old woman!

GAYEV: How's that?

LOPAKHIN: An old woman! (*Starts to go.*)

LYUBOV ANDREYEVNA: (*Startled.*) No, don't go, stay, my dearest, I beg you. Maybe we can think of something.

LOPAKHIN: What's there to think of!

LYUBOV ANDREYEVNA: Don't go, I beg you. It's always more cheerful with you . . . (*Pause.*) I keep expecting something to happen like the house collapsing down around us.

GAYEV: (*Deeply lost in thought.*) A rebound to the corner . . . A spot to the center . . .

LYUBOV ANDREYEVNA: After all, we have sinned so much . . .

LOPAKHIN: What kind of sins could you have . . .

GAYEV: (*Places a fruit-drop in his mouth.*) They say I've eaten up my whole fortune in candy . . . (*Laughs.*)

LYUBOV ANDREYEVNA: Oh, my sins . . . I always squandered my money without holding back, like a madwoman, and I married a man who made no money, only made debts. My husband died of champagne—he drank terribly—and to my misfortune, I fell in love with another man, went off after him, and just then—this was my first punishment, a blow directly to the head—right here in the river . . . My little boy drowned, and I left for abroad, completely left, never to return, never to see this river again . . . I closed my eyes and ran, forgetting myself, and *he* followed me . . . so pitiless, so coarse. I bought a summer house near Mentone, because *he* got sick there, and for three years I knew no rest, day or night. The sick man tortured me, my soul dried up. Then last year, when the summer house was sold to pay the debts, I left for Paris, and there he robbed me, left me, went off with another woman. I tried to poison myself . . . so stupid, so shameless . . . And suddenly, something began to pull me back to Russia, to my homeland, to my little girl . . . (*Wipes away her tears.*) Oh Lord, Lord, have mercy, forgive me my sins! Don't punish me anymore! (*Takes a telegram out of her pocket.*) I received this today from Paris . . . He asks me to forgive him, he begs me to return . . . (*Tears up the telegram.*) I think I hear music from somewhere. (*Listens.*)

GAYEV: That's our famous Jewish orchestra, you remember. Four violins, a flute, and a double-bass.

LYUBOV ANDREYEVNA: It still exists? We should send for them and give a little party.

LOPAKHIN: (*Listens.*) I don't hear it . . . (*Sings softly.*) "For money the Germans will turn the Russians into French."[26] (*Laughs.*) What a play I saw at the theater yesterday, very funny!

LYUBOV ANDREYEVNA: There was probably nothing funny about it. You shouldn't be looking at plays, but look at yourself more often. How dull all your lives are, how much you talk about unnecessary things.

LOPAKHIN: That's true. I frankly admit, our lives are foolish. (*Pause.*) My father was a peasant, an idiot, didn't understand anything, didn't teach me anything, only beat me when he was drunk, and with a stick too. Actually, I'm a windbag and an idiot. I haven't learned anything, my handwriting is atrocious. I'm ashamed to have people see it. I write like a pig.

LYUBOV ANDREYEVNA: You need to get married, my friend.

LOPAKHIN: Yes . . . That's true.

LYUBOV ANDREYEVNA: To our Varya. She's a good girl.

LOPAKHIN: Yes.

LYUBOV ANDREYEVNA: She came to me from simple people, works all day long, and the main thing is that she loves you. Yes, and you've liked her for a long time too.

LOPAKHIN: Well? I'm not against it . . . She's a good girl. (*Pause.*)

GAYEV: They offered me a position in the bank. Six thousand a year . . . Did you hear?

LYUBOV ANDREYEVNA: Oh, you just stay put!

Firs enters; he carries a coat.

FIRS: (*To Gayev.*) Would you please put this on, sir. It's damp out here.

GAYEV: (*Puts on the coat.*) You bore me, old man.

FIRS: Never mind . . . You left this morning without telling me. (*Looks Gayev over.*)

LYUBOV ANDREYEVNA: How old you've gotten, Firs!

FIRS: Excuse me?

---

26. It was said that Russia took its government from the Germans and its culture from the French.

LOPAKHIN: She said, "How very old you've gotten!"

FIRS: I've lived a long time. They wanted to marry me off before your papa was even born . . . (*Laughs.*) When they set us free,[27] I was already a senior valet. But I didn't agree to freedom, stayed with the masters . . . (*Pause.*) I remember everyone was glad for some reason, but why they were glad, they didn't know.

LOPAKHIN: It was so very good in the old days. They flogged you at least.

FIRS: (*Who has not heard.*) I should think so. The peasants and the masters, the masters and the peasants, but now everything's mixed up, you can't understand anything.

GAYEV: Be quiet, Firs. Tomorrow I have to go into the city. I'm supposed to meet a certain general who can give me a promissory note.

LOPAKHIN: Nothing will come of it. And you won't pay the interest, don't worry.

LYUBOV ANDREYEVNA: He's delirious. There are no generals.

Enter Trofimov, Anya, and Varya.

GAYEV: Here come our dear ones.

ANYA: Mama's sitting over here.

LYUBOV ANDREYEVNA: (*Tenderly.*) Come here, come here . . . my own dear family . . . (*Hugs Anya and Varya.*) If only you both knew how I love you. Sit down next to me, right here. (*They sit down.*)

LOPAKHIN: Our eternal student always walks with the ladies.

TROFIMOV: It's none of your business.

LOPAKHIN: He'll soon be fifty years old, and he's still a student.

TROFIMOV: Cut out your stupid jokes.

LOPAKHIN: What's the matter, you freak, are you angry?

---

27. In 1861 Alexander II signed Russia's emancipation act, which abolished landowners' right to own "serfs," also called "souls." However, because no clear arrangements were made to redistribute land, freed serfs often found themselves destitute.

TROFIMOV: Just drop it!

LOPAKHIN: (*Laughs.*) If I may ask, what do you think of me?

TROFIMOV: This is what I think of you, Yermolay Alekseyevich: you are a rich man, soon you will be a millionaire. And, given the balance of nature, you are necessary, like the beast of prey who devours everything that gets in his way, that's how you are necessary. (*All laugh.*)

VARYA: Petya, you would do better to discuss the planets.

LYUBOV ANDREYEVNA: No, let's continue yesterday's conversation.

TROFIMOV: What was it about?

GAYEV: About taking pride in the fact that we are human beings.

TROFIMOV: Yesterday we talked for a long time, but we didn't get anywhere. In human pride, in your idea of it, there is something mystical. And maybe from your vantage point you're right. But when you analyze it simply, without overcomplicating it, what kind of pride can there be, what sense does it make, in light of the fact that human beings are by constitution physiologically weak, that in the vast majority of cases, people are coarse, unintelligent, deeply unhappy? One must stop admiring oneself. One must only work.

GAYEV: You'll still die.

TROFIMOV: Who knows? And what does that mean—you'll die? It may be that people have one hundred senses and that with death only the five known to us are destroyed, but the other ninety-five live on.

LYUBOV ANDREYEVNA: How intelligent you are, Petya! . . .

LOPAKHIN: (*Ironically.*) Extremely intelligent!

TROFIMOV: Humanity moves forward, perfecting its powers. Everything that seems unattainable now, will some day be within our grasp, comprehensible. Only now we must work, and with all our power help those who search for truth. Very few of us in Russia work now. The vast majority of the intelligentsia that I know, don't search for anything, don't do anything and aren't capable of labor. They call themselves the intelligentsia, but they talk to their servants like children, and talk to their peasants as if they were animals, they're poorly educated, don't read anything serious, do absolutely nothing, only talk about science, and understand very little about art. They're all so serious, they all have stern faces, they all talk about what's important, they philosophize, but meanwhile, before their very eyes, the workers eat disgustingly, sleep without pillows, thirty or forty in a single room, everywhere there are bedbugs, stench, dampness, immorality . . . So, apparently, all these good conversations we have, serve only to delude ourselves and others. Show me where the nurseries are that we talk about so much and so often. Where are the libraries? They're found only in novels, but they don't exist in fact. There's only filth, vulgarity, asiaticism[28] . . . I don't like, I'm afraid of these serious physiognomies, I'm afraid of serious conversations. It's better to keep quiet.

LOPAKHIN: Do you know, I get up at five o'clock in the morning, I work from morning to night, and I deal constantly with money, my own and other people's, and so I see what kind of people there are in the world. You only have to start to work at something to understand how few honorable, respectable people there are. One time, when I couldn't sleep, I thought, "Lord, you gave us vast forests, boundless fields, broad horizons, and living here, we really ought to be giants . . ."

LYUBOV ANDREYEVNA: Now you want giants . . . They're only good in fairy tales, otherwise they frighten you.

Yepikhodov crosses upstage and softly, sadly plays the guitar.

LYUBOV ANDREYEVNA: (*Lost in thought.*) There's Yepikhodov . . .

ANYA: (*Lost in thought.*) There's Yepikhodov . . .

GAYEV: The sun has set, ladies and gentlemen.

TROFIMOV: Yes.

GAYEV: (*Not loudly, but as if declaiming.*) Oh, nature, divine nature, you shine with an eternal radiance, beautiful and indifferent, you, whom we call Mother, contain within you both being and death, you give life and you destroy . . .

VARYA: (*Pleadingly.*) Uncle dear!

ANYA: Uncle, you're at it again!

---

28. A commonly used racial pejorative for Russians, whose vast country extends into Central Asia.

TROFIMOV: You'd do better to shoot the green ball to the center with a rebound.

GAYEV: I'll keep quiet, I'll keep quiet.

Everyone sits lost in thought. Silence. Only the quiet mumbling of Firs is heard. Suddenly there is a faraway sound, as if from the sky, the sound of a snapping string, sad.

LYUBOV ANDREYEVNA: What's that?

LOPAKHIN: I don't know. Somewhere far away in the mines a bucket broke loose. But somewhere very far away.

GAYEV: Maybe it's a bird of some kind . . . like a heron.

TROFIMOV: Or an owl.

LYUBOV ANDREYEVNA: (*Shudders.*) It's unsettling somehow!

Pause.

FIRS: Before the calamity it was like that. An owl screeched, and the samovar[29] hissed without stopping.

GAYEV: Before what calamity?

FIRS: Before they set us free.

Pause.

LYUBOV ANDREYEVNA: Come, let's go, my friends. It's already evening. (*To Anya.*) You have tears in your eyes . . . What's wrong, my little girl? (*Hugs her.*)

ANYA: It's all right, Mama. It's nothing.

TROFIMOV: Someone's coming.

A passerby dressed in a worn white peaked cap and coat appears; he is a little drunk.

PASSERBY: Allow me to ask, can I cross through here to get to the station?

GAYEV: You can. Take this road.

---

29. A metal urn that boils water for making tea.

PASSERBY: I'm sincerely grateful to you. (*Coughing.*) The weather is excellent . . . (*Declaims.*) "Brother, my brother, you suffer . . . Go down to the Volga, whose moaning waters . . ."[30] (*To Varya.*) Mademoiselle, give a hungry Russian thirty kopecks . . . (*Varya is startled and cries out.*)

LOPAKHIN: (*Angrily.*) There's a limit to every impropriety.

LYUBOV ANDREYEVNA: (*Struck dumb.*) Take this . . . Here you . . . (*Searches in her purse.*) There's no silver . . . It's all the same, here's a gold piece for you . . .

PASSERBY: I'm sincerely grateful to you! (*Exits.*)

Laughter.

VARYA: (*Startled.*) I'm going . . . I'm going . . . Ah, Mamochka, there's nothing for the servants to eat at home, and you give him gold.

LYUBOV ANDREYEVNA: What can you do with me, I'm so stupid! When we get home, I'll give you everything, everything I have. Yermolay Alekseyevich, lend me some more! . . .

LOPAKHIN: I obey.

LYUBOV ANDREYEVNA: Let's go, ladies and gentlemen, it's time. And Varya, we've made a match for you. Congratulations!

VARYA: (*Through tears.*) Mama, you musn't joke about that.

LOPAKHIN: Ohmelia, get thee to a hermitage . . .[31]

GAYEV: My hands are trembling; I haven't played billiards in a long time.

LOPAKHIN: Ohmelia, oh, nymph, remember me in thy prayers!

LYUBOV ANDREYEVNA: Let's go, ladies and gentlemen. Soon it will be dinner time.

VARYA: He frightened me. My heart's pounding.

LOPAKHIN: Let me remind you, ladies and gentlemen: on August 22nd the cherry orchard will be sold. Think about that! . . . Think about it! . . .

---

30. These lines are from two different Populist poems from the 1870s: the first by Semyon Yakovlevich Nadson (1862–1887) and the second by Nikolay Alekseyevich Nekrasov (1821–1878).

31. Here and below are misquotations from Shakespeare's *Hamlet*, Act III, scene 1, when Prince Hamlet confronts and spurns Ophelia.

All exit except Trofimov and Anya.

ANYA: (*Laughing.*) Thanks to the passerby who frightened Varya, we're alone now.

TROFIMOV: Varya's afraid that we will suddenly fall in love with one another, so she follows us about all day long. With her narrow mind, she can't understand that we are above love. To avoid the petty and illusionary that interferes with our being free and happy, that is the goal and meaning of our lives. Forward! We are going irresistibly toward a bright star which shines in the distance! Forward! Don't lag behind, my friends!

ANYA: (*Clasping her hands.*) How well you speak! (*Pause.*) It's divine here today!

TROFIMOV: Yes, the weather is amazing.

ANYA: What have you done to me, Petya, that I don't love the cherry orchard as I did before? I loved it so tenderly, I thought there wasn't a better place in the whole world than our orchard.

TROFIMOV: All Russia is our orchard. The world is big and beautiful, and there are many wonderful places in it. (*Pause.*) Just think, Anya, your grandfather and great-grandfather, and all your ancestors were serf-owners, owners of living souls. So isn't it possible that behind each cherry tree in the orchard, behind each leaf, behind each trunk, there are human beings looking out at you? Isn't it possible that you could hear their voices? To own living souls—surely that has transformed all of you, those who lived before and those who live now, so that your mother, you, your uncle don't even notice that you are living in debt, at someone else's expense, at the expense of those people who weren't allowed to go further than your threshold . . . We lag behind by at least two hundred years, we have exactly nothing, no definite relationship to the past, we only philosophize, complain about boredom and drink vodka. Isn't it clear that to start to live in the present, we must begin to atone for our past, to finish with it? And only suffering can atone for it, only extraordinary, ceaseless labor. Remember that, Anya.

ANYA: The house in which we live has not been our house for a long time, and I'll leave, I give you my word.

TROFIMOV: If you have the keys to the household, throw them away, into the well, and leave. Be free like the wind.

ANYA: (*In ecstasy.*) How well you speak!

TROFIMOV: Believe me, Anya, believe me! I'm not yet thirty. I'm young, still a student, but I've already endured so much! As soon as it's winter, I'm hungry, sick, worried, poor like a beggar, and wherever fate has driven me, there I've gone! But still my soul has always, at every moment of the day and night, been full of inexplicable premonitions. I have a premonition of happiness, Anya! I can already see it . . .

ANYA: (*Lost in thought.*) The moon is rising.

Yepikhodov is heard still playing the same sad song on the guitar. The moon rises. Somewhere near the poplars, Varya looks for Anya and calls, "Anya! Where are you?"

TROFIMOV: Yes, the moon is rising. (*Pause.*) Happiness, too, is rising, getting nearer and nearer, I already hear its footsteps. And if we don't see it, don't know it, what of it! Others will see it!

The voice of Varya: "Anya! Where are you?"

TROFIMOV: It's Varya again! (*Angrily.*) It's revolting!

ANYA: Well then, let's go to the river! It's nice there.

TROFIMOV: Let's go. (*They go.*)

The voice of Varya: "Anya! Anya!"

Curtain.

Act III

A drawing room, separated from a hall by an archway. The chandelier is lit. The Jewish orchestra, the same one mentioned in Act II, is heard playing in the anteroom. Evening. They are dancing a *grand rond* in the hall. The voice of Simeonov-Pishchik: *Promenade à une paire!* Entering into the drawing room: the first couple—Pishchik and Charlotta Ivanovna; the second—Trofimov and Lyubov Andreyevna; the third—Anya with a postal clerk, the fourth—Varya with the station master, etc. Varya cries quietly and, while dancing, wipes away her tears. Dunyasha is in the last couple to enter. They all go through the drawing room, Pishchik yells: *Grand rond, balancez!* and *Les cavaliers à genoux et remerciez vos dames!*[32] Firs in a frock coat[33] brings in a tray with seltzer water. Pishchik and Trofimov enter the drawing room.

PISHCHIK: I'm full-blooded, but I've already had two strokes, so it's hard for me to dance. But, as they say, when in Rome, do as the Romans do. I'm as healthy as a horse. Concerning our origins, my late parent—what a joker he was, may he rest in peace—said that the ancient line of the Simeonov-Pishchiks comes down from that very same horse that Caligula seated in the senate[34] . . . (*Sits down.*) But then, the trouble is: there's no money! A hungry dog believes only in meat . . . (*Snores and then wakes up again.*) Same with me . . . I can only think about money . . .

TROFIMOV: There is actually something horse-like about your figure . . .

PISHCHIK: Well . . . A horse is a good animal . . . You can sell a horse . . .

In the neighboring room a billiard game can be heard.
Varya appears in the hall, under the arch.

TROFIMOV: (*Teases Varya.*) *Madame* Lopakhin! *Madame* Lopakhin! . . .

VARYA: (*Angrily.*) "Shabby lord!"

TROFIMOV: Yes, I'm shabby, and proud of it!

VARYA: (*Having bitter second thoughts.*) We've hired musicians, but what can we pay them with? (*Exits.*)

TROFIMOV: (*To Pishchik.*) If you had used all the energy you spent all your life in pursuit of money to pay the interest on your

---

32. They are dancing a quadrille (similar to a square dance), and Pishchik is calling out the steps in French: "Promenade with your partner!"; "In a large circle, step from side to side!"; "Gentlemen, on your knees to thank your ladies!"

33. A man's dress jacket that is fitted at the waist and extends to the knees.

34. The ancient Roman emperor Caligula (12–41 C.E.), thought to be insane, mocked the Senate by making his horse a member.

loan, if you had used that energy for something else, then you probably could have moved the earth.

PISHCHIK: Nietzsche . . . the philosopher . . . the greatest, the most famous . . . a man with a huge mind, says in his essays, that you can make counterfeit money.[35]

TROFIMOV: You've read Nietzsche?

PISHCHIK: Well . . . Dashenka told me. And now I'm in such straits that I'm ready to make some . . . The day after tomorrow I have to pay three hundred and ten rubles . . . I've already got together one hundred and thirty . . . (*Feels his pocket, anxiously.*) The money's gone! I've lost the money! (*Through tears.*) Where's the money? (*Joyfully.*) Here it is, in the lining . . . I even broke out into a sweat . . .

Enter Lyubov Andreyevna and Charlotta Ivanovna.

LYUBOV ANDREYEVNA: (*Humming the lezginka.*[36]) Why is Leonid taking so long? What is he doing in town? (*To Dunyasha.*) Dunyasha, offer the musicians some tea . . .

TROFIMOV: The auction probably didn't take place yet.

LYUBOV ANDREYEVNA: The musicians came at the wrong time, and we gave a ball at the wrong time . . . Well, never mind . . . (*Sits and softly sings.*)

CHARLOTTA: (*Gives Pishchik a deck of cards.*) Here's a deck of cards for you. Think of a card, any card.

PISHCHIK: Got it!

CHARLOTTA: Now shuffle the deck. Very good. Give it to me, oh my dear *Herr* Pishchik. *Ein, zwei, drei!*[37] Now, take a look. The card is in your side pocket . . .

PISHCHIK: (*Pulls a card out of his side pocket.*) The eight of spades, that's exactly right! (*Surprised.*) Imagine that!

CHARLOTTA: (*Holds the deck of cards in her hand, to Trofimov.*) Tell me quick, which card is on top.

---

35. The philosopher Friedrich Nietzsche (1844–1900) saw Western civilization as *Beyond Good and Evil* (the title of his book from 1886).
36. A lively sword dance from the Caucasus.
37. "Mr. Pishchik"; "one, two, three" (German).

TROFIMOV: What? Well, the queen of spades.

CHARLOTTA: Here it is! (*To Pishchik*.) Well? Which card is on the bottom?

PISHCHIK: The ace of hearts.

CHARLOTTA: Here it is! (*Strikes her palm, the deck disappears.*) What beautiful weather we have today! (*A mysterious feminine voice, apparently coming from under the floor answers her: "Oh yes, the weather is splendid, my lady."*) You are so very nice, my pretty one, my ideal . . . (*The voice: "And you, my lady, I like you very much too."*)

STATION MASTER: (*Applauding.*) Madam the ventriloquist, bravo!

PISHCHIK: (*Surprised.*) Imagine that! My most charming Charlotta Ivanovna . . . I'm simply in love . . .

CHARLOTTA: In love? (*Shrugs her shoulders.*) Can you love? *Guter mensch aber schlecter musikant.*[38]

TROFIMOV: (*Clasps Pishchik on the shoulder.*) Just like a horse . . .

CHARLOTTA: Attention please, one more trick. (*Takes a lap robe off a chair.*) Here's a very pretty plaid, I would like to sell it . . . (*Shakes it out and holds it up.*) Doesn't anyone want to buy it?

PISHCHIK: (*Surprised.*) Imagine that!

CHARLOTTA: *Ein, zwei, drei!* (*Quickly raises the lap robe; behind it stands Anya to the amazement of all; she curtsies, runs to her mother, hugs her, and runs out into the hall.*)

LYUBOV ANDREYEVNA: (*Applauds.*) Bravo, bravo! . . .

CHARLOTTA: Now one more! *Ein, zwei, drei!* (*Raises the lap robe; behind it stands Varya, who bows.*)

PISHCHIK: (*Surprised.*) Imagine that!

CHARLOTTA: The end! (*Throws the lap robe to Pishchik, curtsies, and runs out into the hall.*)

PISHCHIK: (*Hurries after her.*) You are a sorceress . . . That's what you are! You are! (*Exits.*)

---

38. "A good man, but a poor musician" (German).

LYUBOV ANDREYEVNA: But Leonid's not back yet. What is he doing in town so long? I don't understand! Shouldn't everything there be finished by now? The estate is either sold or the auction didn't take place. Why prolong the suspense!

VARYA: (*Trying to calm her.*) Uncle bought it, I'm sure of it.

TROFIMOV: (*Mockingly.*) Sure.

VARYA: Our great aunt sent him her power of attorney to buy it and transfer the debt to her name. She did it for Anya. And I'm sure, with God's help, Uncle is buying it.

LYUBOV ANDREYEVNA: Your great aunt from Yaroslavl sent fifteen thousand to buy the estate in her name—she doesn't trust us—and that's not enough money to pay even the interest on the mortgage. (*Covers her face with her hands.*) Today my fate is decided, my fate . . .

TROFIMOV: (*Teasing Varya.*) *Madame* Lopakhin!

VARYA: (*Angrily.*) Eternal student! They've already thrown you out of the university twice.

LYUBOV ANDREYEVNA: Why are you angry, Varya? He teases you about Lopakhin, but so what? Marry Lopakhin, if you want. He's a good and interesting person. If you don't want to, then don't. No one's forcing you, darling . . .

VARYA: To be honest, Mamochka, I look upon this as a serious matter. He's a good person, I like him.

LYUBOV ANDREYEVNA: So marry him. Why wait? I don't understand!

VARYA: Mamochka, I can't propose to him myself! For two years now, everyone's been talking to me about him, everyone's talking but him. Either he keeps quiet or he jokes. I understand. He's getting rich, he's busy, he has no time for me. If there were some money, even a little, only a hundred rubles, I would quit everything, and move on somewhere. I'd go to a hermitage.

TROFIMOV: How splendid!

VARYA: (*To Trofimov.*) A student should be smart! (*In a softer tone of voice, with tears in her eyes.*) How ugly you've gotten, Petya! How old! (*To Lyubov Andreyevna, no longer crying.*) It's just that I can't live without something to keep me busy, Mamochka. I need to be doing something every minute.

Yasha enters.

YASHA: (*Barely holding back his laugher.*) Yepikhodov broke a billiard cue! . . . (*Exits.*)

VARYA: Why is Yepikhodov here? Who let him play billiards? I don't understand these people . . . (*Exits.*)

LYUBOV ANDREYEVNA: Don't tease her, Petya. You can see that she's miserable even without that.

TROFIMOV: But she's very eager to meddle in other people's business. All summer long she didn't give me or Anya any peace; she was so afraid a little romance would develop between us. What business is that of hers? And besides I've never given that impression, I'm far away from such vulgarity. We are above love!

LYUBOV ANDREYEVNA: And so then I must be below love. (*In great agitation.*) Why is Leonid not here? If only I knew whether the estate were sold or not? This trouble seems to me so unbelievable that I don't even know what to think, I'm in despair . . . I could scream right now . . . could do something stupid. Save me, Petya. Tell me something, tell me . . .

TROFIMOV: Whether the estate has been sold today or whether it hasn't been sold—isn't it all the same? It was finished long ago, there's no turning back, the path is overgrown. Be calm, dear soul. You don't need to deceive yourself, you need to look truth straight in the eye.

LYUBOV ANDREYEVNA: What truth? You can see what is true and what is not true, but I feel like I've lost my sight and can see nothing. You boldly decide how to answer all the important questions, but tell me, dear friend, isn't that because you're young, and because you haven't yet suffered through any one of those questions? You look boldly forward, but isn't that because you don't see, you don't expect anything frightening there, since life is still hidden from your young eyes? You're bolder, more honorable, deeper than us, but just think, be a tiny little bit more generous, and spare me. I was born here, after all, lived here with my father and mother, my grandfather . . . I love this house. Without the cherry orchard I wouldn't understand my own life, and if it must be sold, then sell me with the orchard . . . (*Hugs Trofimov, kisses him on the forehead.*) My son drowned here, after all . . . (*Cries.*) Pity me, my good, my kind friend.

TROFIMOV: You know that I sympathize wholeheartedly.

LYUBOV ANDREYEVNA: But you should say that differently, differently . . . (*Takes out a handkerchief, and a telegram falls to the floor.*) My soul feels so heavy today, you can't imagine. Here it's noisy, but my soul trembles with every sound, I'm trembling all over, but I can't go to my room, it's frightening to sit by myself in the quiet. Don't judge me, Petya . . . I love you, like my own son. I would gladly give you Anya's hand, I swear it, but dear friend, you must learn, you must finish your studies. You don't do anything, you let fate toss you from place to place, it's so strange . . . Isn't that true? Isn't it? And you must do something with that beard, so it will grow . . . (*Laughs.*) You're ridiculous!

TROFIMOV: (*Picks up the telegram.*) I don't want to be a beauty.

LYUBOV ANDREYEVNA: The telegram's from Paris. Every day I get one. Yesterday and today. That wild man is sick again, things aren't going well for him again . . . He begs me to forgive him, implores me to come back, and really I ought to go to Paris to be with him. You look so stern, Petya, but what can I do, my friend, what can I do, he's sick, he's alone, unhappy, and who's there to look after him, who'll keep him from making mistakes, who'll give him his medicine? And why should I hide it, or keep quiet about it? I love him, that's obvious. I love him, love him . . . It's a stone around my neck, and it's pulling me down to the bottom, but I love this stone, I can't live without him. (*Presses Trofimov's hand.*) Don't think badly of me, Petya, and don't tell me anything, don't tell me . . .

TROFIMOV: (*Through tears.*) Forgive me for my frankness, for God's sake, but didn't he rob you?

LYUBOV ANDREYEVNA: No, no, no, don't talk like that . . . (*Covers her ears.*)

TROFIMOV: But he's a scoundrel. And you're the only one who doesn't know it! He's a petty scoundrel, a nonentity . . .

LYUBOV ANDREYEVNA: (*Getting angry but controlling it.*) You are twenty-six or twenty-seven years old, and you're still a schoolboy in the second grade!

TROFIMOV: Let me be!

LYUBOV ANDREYEVNA: You must become a man, at your age you should understand those who love. And you yourself must love . . . You must fall in love! (*Angrily.*) Yes, yes! You have no purity, you're only a prude, a ridiculous freak, ugly . . .

TROFIMOV: (*In horror.*) What is she saying!

LYUBOV ANDREYEVNA: "I'm above love!" You're not above love, as Firs would say, you're just a "nincompoop." At your age not to have a lover! . . .

TROFIMOV: (*In terror.*) That's horrible! What is she saying?! (*Goes quickly toward the hall, holding his head in his hands.*) That's horrible . . . I can't stand it, I'm going . . . (*Exits but returns immediately.*) Everything is finished between us! (*Goes out into the anteroom.*)

LYUBOV ANDREYEVNA: (*Yells after him.*) Petya, wait a minute! You're ridiculous, I was joking! Petya!

He is heard quickly going down the stairs, then suddenly he falls down with a clatter. Anya and Varya cry out, and then laughter is heard.

LYUBOV ANDREYEVNA: What was that?

Anya runs in.

ANYA: (*Laughing.*) Petya fell down the stairs. (*She runs out.*)

LYUBOV ANDREYEVNA: What a freak Petya is . . .

The station master stands in the middle of the hall and recites "The Sinful Woman," a poem by A. Tolstóy.[39] Everyone listens to him, but he has finished only a few lines when

39. "The Sinful Woman" is a poem by Aleksey Konstantinovich Tolstoy (1817–1875), a cousin of the novelist. It tells the biblical story of the prostitute Mary Magdalene, who repents when she meets Jesus at a celebratory feast. In production, the first lines can be used:
    The lute resounds, the cymbals crash!
    Amidst the twirling dancers,
    Dressed in rich brocades, her dark eyes flash!
    Near the portal regally stand
    A pair of broken columns,
    Where flowers too are strewn . . .

waltz music is heard coming from the anteroom and the recitation breaks off. Everyone dances. Trofimov, Anya, Varya, and Lyubov Andreyevna come in from the anteroom.

LYUBOV ANDREYEVNA: Well Petya . . . Well, dear heart . . . Please forgive me. Let's dance . . . (*Dances with Petya.*)

> *Anya and Varya dance. Firs enters and places his cane next to the side door. Yasha also comes into the drawing room and watches the dance.*

YASHA: What's up, Grandpa?

FIRS: Don't feel well. Before this, generals, barons, admirals used to dance at our balls, but now we send for a postal clerk and the station master, and even they don't feel much like coming. Somehow I've gotten weak. The late master, their grandfather, used to use sealing wax for all our diseases. I've been taking sealing wax every day now for about twenty years, or maybe more. Maybe that's why I'm alive.

YASHA: You bore me, Grandpa. (*Yawns.*) Hope you croak soon.

FIRS: Ah, you . . . nincompoop! (*Mumbles.*)

> *Trofimov and Lyubov Andreyevna dance into the hall, then into the drawing room.*

LYUBOV ANDREYEVNA: *Merci.*[40] I'll sit for awhile . . . (*Sits down.*) I'm tired.

> *Anya enters.*

ANYA: (*Excited.*) There was some man in the kitchen just now who said that the cherry orchard was sold today.

LYUBOV ANDREYEVNA: Sold to whom?

ANYA: He didn't say to whom. He left. (*Dances with Trofimov, and they exit into the hall.*)

YASHA: That was just some old man babbling. A stranger.

---

40. "Thank you" (French).

FIRS: And Leonid Andreyevich still isn't here, he didn't come back yet. He wore a light spring coat, and just you wait, he'll catch his death of cold. Ah, young and green!

LYUBOV ANDREYEVNA: I'll die right now. Go, Yasha, find out who it was sold to.

YASHA: But he left a long time ago, that old man. (*Laughs.*)

LYUBOV ANDREYEVNA: (*Slightly annoyed.*) Well, what are you laughing at? Why are you so happy?

YASHA: That Yepikhodov is very funny. An empty-headed person, Twenty-Two Troubles.

LYUBOV ANDREYEVNA: Firs, if they sell the estate, where will you go?

FIRS: Wherever you say, there I'll go.

LYUBOV ANDREYEVNA: Why does your face look like that? Are you ill? You should go to sleep, you know . . .

FIRS: Yes . . . (*With a smile.*) I'll go to sleep, and then without me who will serve, who will keep things in order? I'm the only one in the whole house.

YASHA: (*To Lyubov Andreyevna.*) Lyubov Andreyevna! Allow me to make a request of you, be so kind! If you go to Paris again, take me with you, do me this kindness. It's absolutely impossible for me to stay here. (*Looks around, in a whisper.*) I don't need to tell you, you can see for yourself, the country's uneducated, the people are immoral, then there's the boredom. In the kitchen they feed us atrociously, and then there's this Firs always walking around, mumbling various irrelevant things. Take me with you, be so kind!

Pishchik enters.

PISHCHIK: May I have the pleasure . . . of a little waltz, my most beauteous lady . . . (*Lyubov Andreyevna follows him.*) My charmer, I still need to borrow one hundred and eighty little rubles from you . . . I'll borrow . . . (*They dance.*) One hundred and eighty little rubles . . . (*They exit into the hall.*)

YASHA: (*Softly sings.*) "I wonder if you understand the beating of my heart . . ."[41]

41. From a popular ballad of the 1870s.

In the hall, a figure in a gray top hat and checked pants waves a hand and jumps. There are cries of "Bravo, Charlotta Ivanovna!"

DUNYASHA: (*Stops in order to powder her nose.*) The mistress told me to dance. There are so many cavaliers, but so few ladies, and now my head is spinning from the dances, my heart is pounding, Firs Nikolayevich. And just now the clerk from the post office said something to me that took my breath away.

The music quiets down.

FIRS: What did he say to you?

DUNYASHA: "You," he said, "are like a flower."

YASHA: (*Yawns.*) Ignoramus . . . (*Exits.*)

DUNYASHA: "Like a flower" . . . I'm such a delicate young girl, I love tender words so awfully much.

FIRS: You've got your head screwed on wrong.

Enter Yepikhovdov.

YEPIKHODOV: Avdotya Fyodorovna, you don't want to see me . . . I might as well be some kind of an insect. (*Sighs.*) Ah, life!

DUNYASHA: What do you want?

YEPIKHODOV: Undoubtedly, you are perhaps right. (*Sighs.*) But, of course, if you look at it from a point of view, if I may express myself this way, forgive me for my frankness, you have brought me to a state of mind. I know my own fortune, every day something bad happens to me, and I've been used to it for a long time now, and so I look at my fate with a smile. You gave me your word, and although I . . .

DUNYASHA: I beg you, let's talk about this later; leave me in peace now. Now I'm daydreaming . . . (*Plays with her fan.*)

YEPIKHODOV: Something bad happens to me every day, and if I may express myself, I only smile, I even laugh.

Varya enters from the hall.

VARYA: (*To Yepikhodov.*) You still haven't left, Semyon? What a disrespectful man you are, truly. (*To Dunyasha.*) Run along,

Dunyasha. (*To Yepikhodov.*) You either play billiards and break the cues, or you walk around the drawing room like a guest.

YEPIKHODOV: You cannot, if I may express myself, you cannot reproach me.

VARYA: I'm not reproaching you, I'm telling you. You're the only one who knows why you walk from place to place, and don't attend to your business. We keep a clerk, but who knows what for.

YEPIKHODOV: (*Offended.*) About whether I work, whether I walk around, whether I eat, whether I play billiards, only people who understand and are older can judge.

VARYA: You dare to talk to me like that! (*Flaring up.*) You dare? You mean to say that I don't understand anything? Get out of here! This minute.

YEPIKHODOV: (*Losing his courage.*) I beg you to express yourself in a more delicate way.

VARYA: (*Losing her temper.*) Get out of here this minute! Out! (*He goes to the door; she follows him.*) Twenty-Two Troubles! Don't let me see your face! Don't let me hear your voice! (*Yepikhodov exits. His voice behind the door: "I'll complain about you . . ."*) Are you coming back? (*She takes the cane which Firs left near the door.*) Come on . . . Come on . . . Come on, I'll show you . . . Well are you coming? Are you coming? Then take this . . . (*She brandishes the cane and at the same time, Lopakhin enters.*)

LOPAKHIN: Thank you kindly.

VARYA: (*Angrily and mockingly.*) My fault!

LOPAKHIN: It's nothing, madam. I humbly thank you for your pleasant hospitality.

VARYA: Don't bother to thank me. (*Walks away, then looks around and asks gently.*) I didn't hurt you, did I?

LOPAKHIN: No, not at all. A huge bump's coming up, that's all.

A voice in the hall: "Lopakhin's arrived!
It's Yermolay Alekseyevich!"

PISHCHIK: (*Enters.*) A sight for sore eyes . . . (*Kisses Lopakhin.*) You smell of cognac, my dear, my darling. We've been making merry here too.

Lyubov Andreyevna enters.

LYUBOV ANDREYEVNA: Is it you, Yermolay Alekseyevich? Why did it take you so long? Where's Leonid?

LOPAKHIN: Leonid Andreyevich arrived with me, he's coming . . .

LYUBOV ANDREYEVNA: (*Excited.*) Well, what happened? Was there an auction? Tell me!

LOPAKHIN: (*Confused, afraid to destroy his own joy.*) The auction was over at four o'clock . . . We missed the train, had to wait until nine thirty. (*Sighs deeply.*) Ugh! My head is spinning a little . . .

Gayev enters; in his right hand he has some purchases, with his left he wipes away his tears.

LYUBOV ANDREYEVNA: Lyonya, what is it? Lyonya, what? (*Impatiently, with tears in her eyes.*) Quickly, for God's sake . . .

GAYEV: (*Doesn't answer her, only waves his hand; to Firs, crying.*) Here take this . . . There's some anchovies, Kerch herring[42] . . . I didn't eat anything today . . . How much I've suffered! (*The door to the billiard room is open; the striking of balls can be heard, and the voice of Yasha: "Seven and eighteen!" Gayev's expression changes; he's no longer crying.*) I'm awfully tired. Help me, Firs, to get undressed. (*Exits to his room, Firs following him.*)

PISHCHIK: What happened at the auction? Tell me!

LYUBOV ANDREYEVNA: Was the cherry orchard sold?

LOPAKHIN: It was sold.

LYUBOV ANDREYEVNA: Who bought it?

LOPAKHIN: I bought it. (*Pause.*)

---

42. A seafood delicacy from the Ukraine.

*Lyubov Andreyevna is overcome; she would fall if
she weren't standing near an armchair or table. Varya
takes the keys from her belt, throws them on the floor
in the middle of the drawing room and exits.*

LOPAKHIN: I bought it! Wait a minute, ladies and gentlemen, be so
kind, my head is swimming, I can't talk . . . (*Laughs.*) We got
to the auction. Deriganov was there. Leonid Andreyevich had
only fifteen thousand and Deriganov had already put down
thirty thousand over and above the debt. I saw how the business stood, so I jumped in and put down forty . . . He put
down forty-five. I made it fifty-five. You see he kept adding five
thousand and I added ten each time . . . Well, it came to a finish. I put down ninety thousand over and above the debt, and
it was mine. Now the cherry orchard is mine! Mine! (*Laughs
out loud.*) My God, Lord in Heaven, the cherry orchard is
mine! Tell me that I'm drunk, not in my right mind, that I've
imagined all of this . . . (*Stamps his feet.*) Don't laugh at me.
If my father and grandfather were to get up out of their graves
and look at everything that's happened, how their Yermolay,
their beaten, half-literate Yermolay, who ran around barefoot
in the winter, how this very same Yermolay bought an estate,
the most beautiful one in the whole world. I bought the estate
where my grandfather and father were slaves, where they
weren't allowed into the kitchen. I'm asleep, this is a mirage
for me, it only seems to be . . . This is the fruit of your imagi-
nation, hidden by the darkness of the unknown . . . (*Picks up
the keys, smiling tenderly.*) She threw down the keys, wants
to show that she's no longer the housekeeper here . . . (*Jingles
the keys.*) Well, it's all the same. (*The orchestra is heard tun-
ing up.*) Hey musicians, play, I want to hear you! Everyone,
come look at how Yermolay Lopakhin will take the axe to the
cherry orchard, how the trees will fall to the ground! We'll
build summer houses and our grandchildren and their grandchildren will see a new life . . . Music, play! (*The music plays.
Lyubov Andreyevna lowers herself to a chair and bitterly
cries. To her reproachfully.*) Why, why didn't you listen to me?
My poor, good woman, you can't go back now. (*With tears.*)
Oh if only all this would pass quickly, if only our incoherent,
unhappy lives would change quickly!

PISHCHIK: (*Takes him by the arm, in a whisper.*) She's crying. Let's go into the hall, leave her alone . . . Let's go . . . (*Takes him by the arm and leads him into the hall.*)

LOPAKHIN: What happened? Music, play out clearly! Let everything be as I want! (*With irony.*) The new landowner is coming; the owner of the cherry orchard! (*Accidentally bumps into a table which almost knocks over a candelabra.*) I can pay for everything! (*Exits with Pishchik.*)

There is no one in the hall and drawing room except Lyubov Andreyevna, who sits huddled up, and weeps bitterly. The music plays softly. Quickly Anya and Trofimov enter. Anya goes to her mother and kneels in front of her. Trofimov remains at the entrance to the hall.

ANYA: Mama! . . . Mama, are you crying? My dear, kind, my good Mama, my beautiful Mama, I love you . . . I bless you. The cherry orchard is sold, it's gone, that's true, true, but don't cry, Mama, your life remains ahead of you, your good, pure soul remains . . . Come with me away from here, my darling, come! . . . We'll plant a new orchard, more luxurious than this one, you'll see, you'll understand, and joy, quiet deep joy will fill your soul, like the rays of the setting sun, and you'll smile, Mama! Come, darling! Come! . . .

Curtain.

Act IV

The set from the first Act. There are no curtains in the windows, or paintings on the walls, there is a little furniture remaining which is pushed to one corner, as if to be sold. There is a feeling of emptiness. Near the door to the outside and upstage there are suitcases, traveling bundles, etc. To the left, the door is open, and from there the voices of Varya and Anya are heard. Lopakhin stands and waits. Yasha holds a tray with glasses, filled with champagne. In the hallway, Yepikhodov ties up a box. Far offstage there is a rumbling. The peasants are saying goodbye. The voice of Gayev: "Thank you, my friends, thank you."

YASHA: The simple people have come to say goodbye. I am of the opinion, Yermolay Alekseyevich, they're a good people but they don't understand much.

*The rumbling quiets down. Lyubov Andreyevna and
Gayev enter from the hallway; she does not cry, but she
is pale, her lips are trembling, she cannot speak.*

GAYEV: You gave them your purse, Lyuba. You musn't do that! You musn't do that!

LYUBOV ANDREYEVNA: I couldn't help it! I couldn't help it! (*They both exit.*)

LOPAKHIN: (*At the door, after them.*) Please, I most humbly beg you! Have a drink to our goodbyes. I didn't think to bring any from town and I only found one bottle at the station. Please! (*Pause.*) What's wrong, ladies and gentlemen! Don't you want to? (*Walks away from the door.*) If I'd known, I wouldn't have brought it. Well, I won't drink any either. (*Yasha carefully puts the tray on the table.*) Drink up, Yasha, you at least have some.

YASHA: To those who are departing! Good luck to those who stay! (*Drinks.*) This isn't real champagne, I can assure you.

LOPAKHIN: Eight rubles a bottle. (*Pause.*) It's cold as hell here.

YASHA: They didn't light the fires, since we're leaving. (*Laughs.*)

LOPAKHIN: What's the matter?

YASHA: Just happy.

LOPAKHIN: Outside it's October, but it's as sunny and as quiet as summer. Good for building. (*Looking at his watch, at the door.*) Ladies and gentlemen, keep in mind that the train leaves in just forty-six minutes! That means, that in twenty minutes you have to leave for the station. So hurry up a bit.

Trofimov in a coat enters from the outside.

TROFIMOV: I think it's already time to leave. The horses are harnessed. The devil knows where my galoshes are. They're gone. (*At the door.*) Anya, my galoshes aren't anywhere! I didn't find them!

LOPAKHIN: And I have to go to Kharkov. I'll go with you on the same train. I'll spend the whole winter in Kharkov. I've been hanging about with you all this time and tormenting myself by staying away from my business. I can't live without work,

I don't know what to do with my hands. They hang about so strangely, as if they belonged to someone else.

TROFIMOV: We'll be leaving and so you can get back to your own useful work again.

LOPAKHIN: Have a quick drink.

TROFIMOV: I can't.

LOPAKHIN: So you'll be going to Moscow now?

TROFIMOV: Yes, I'll take them to town and tomorrow I'll go to Moscow.

LOPAKHIN: Yes . . . Well, the professors, no doubt, haven't been giving their lectures; they're probably all waiting for you to come back!

TROFIMOV: It's none of your business.

LOPAKHIN: How many years have you been studying at the university?

TROFIMOV: Why not think up something a little newer. That's old and flat. (*Looks for his galoshes.*) You know, we may never see each other again, so allow me to give you one piece of advice at parting: don't wave your arms! Get rid of that habit—waving your arms. And this too—building summer houses and counting on the summer folk to cultivate the land on their own—that's waving your arms too . . . But anyway, I still love you. You have fine, tender fingers, like an artist, you have a fine, tender soul . . .

LOPAKHIN: (*Hugs him.*) Goodbye, my friend. Thank you for everything. If you need it, let me give you some money for the road.

TROFIMOV: What for? I don't need it.

LOPAKHIN: But you don't have any!

TROFIMOV: Yes I do. Thank you. I got some for a translation. Here it is, in my pocket. (*Anxiously.*) But my galoshes aren't here.

VARYA: (*From the other room.*) Take these disgusting things! (*She throws a pair of rubber galoshes on stage.*)

TROFIMOV: Why are you angry, Varya? Hmmm . . . These aren't my galoshes!

LOPAKHIN: In the spring I planted two thousand seven hundred acres of poppies and now I've made forty thousand clear profit from them. But when my poppies were in bloom, what a picture that was! So as I said, I made forty thousand and that means I'm offering you a loan because I can. Why turn your nose up at it? I'm a peasant . . . I speak plainly.

TROFIMOV: Your father was a serf, mine—a pharmacist, but that doesn't necessarily mean anything. (*Lopakhin takes out his wallet.*) Put it away, put it away . . . Even if you gave me two hundred thousand, I wouldn't take it. I'm a free man. Everything that all of you, the rich and the poor, value so highly and dearly hasn't the slightest influence over me, it's like fluff blown around by the wind. I can get along without you, I can pass you by, I'm strong and proud. Humanity is going toward the highest truth, toward the highest happiness that is possible on earth, and I am in the front ranks.

LOPAKHIN: Will you get there?

TROFIMOV: I'll get there. (*Pause.*) I'll get there or I'll show others the way to get there.

The sound of the axe chopping down
trees is heard in the distance.

LOPAKHIN: Well, goodbye, my friend. It's time to go. We turn our noses up at each other, but life passes us by unconcerned. When I work for a long time without a break, then my thoughts rest easier, and I think that I too know why I'm living. But, brother, how many people are there in Russia, who live without knowing why. Well, it's all the same, that's not what keeps things going. Leonid Andreyevich, they say, has taken a position, he'll work in the bank, six thousand a year . . . Only he probably won't stick to it, he's very lazy . . .

ANYA: (*At the door.*) Mama asks you not to cut the orchard while she's still here.

TROFIMOV: Really, have you no tact . . . (*Exits through the hallway.*)

LOPAKHIN: Right away, right away . . . These people, really. (*Follows Trofimov off.*)

ANYA: Did they take Firs to the hospital?

YASHA: I told them to this morning. I think they must have taken him.

ANYA: (*To Yepikhodov, who crosses through the hall.*) Semyon Panteleyevich, find out, please, if they took Firs to the hospital.

YASHA: (*Offended.*) I told Yégor to this morning. Why ask about it ten times!

YEPIKHODOV: Long-lived Firs, in my decisive opinion, is not fit to be mended. It is high time for him to join his forefathers. I can only envy him. (*Puts a suitcase down on a hatbox and crushes it.*) There, of course. Just as I knew. (*Exits.*)

YASHA: (*Sarcastically.*) Twenty-Two Troubles.

VARYA: (*Behind the door.*) Did they take Firs to the hospital?

ANYA: They took him.

VARYA: Why didn't they take the letter to the doctor with them?

ANYA: We'll have to send it on after them . . . (*Exits.*)

VARYA: (*From the neighboring room.*) Where's Yasha? Tell him his mother's come to say goodbye to him.

YASHA: (*Waves his arm.*) They are trying my patience.

Dunyasha has been fussing with the baggage the whole time; now, when Yasha is alone, she goes up to him.

DUNYASHA: If only you'd look at me for one more time, Yasha. You're leaving . . . forsaking me . . . (*Cries and throws her arms around him.*)

YASHA: Why cry? (*Drinks champagne.*) In six days I'll be in Paris again. Tomorrow we'll take the express train and off we'll go, you won't see us for the dust. I can hardly believe it. *Vive la France!*[43] . . . This isn't for me, I can't live here. Nothing to do about it. I've looked at these ignoramuses enough—I've had enough! (*Drinks champagne.*) Why cry? Behave yourself properly, and you won't cry.

DUNYASHA: (*Powders her nose, looking in a hand mirror.*) Send me a letter from Paris. After all, I loved you, Yasha, loved you so! I'm a tender creature, Yasha!

43. "Long live France!" (French).

YASHA: They're coming this way! (*Fusses over the suitcases, sings quietly.*)

*Enter Lyubov Andreyevna, Gayev, Anya,
and Charlotta Ivanovna.*

GAYEV: We have to go. Only a little time left. (*Looking at Yasha.*) Who smells of herring?

LYUBOV ANDREYEVNA: In about ten minutes we'll go out to the carriages . . . (*Glances around the room.*) Goodbye, dear house, old grandfather. The winter will pass, then will come spring, and you won't be here anymore, they'll tear you down. How much these walls have seen! (*Kisses her daughter warmly.*) My treasure, you're shining, your eyes are sparkling like diamonds. Are you happy? Very?

ANYA: Very! A new life is beginning, Mama!

GAYEV: (*Happily.*) True, everything's very good now. Before the sale of the cherry orchard, all of us were so worried, we suffered, and then, when the question was finally decided, irrevocably, everyone calmed down, even became happy . . . I'm a banker now, now I'm a financier . . . Yellow ball into the center, and you, Lyuba, somehow you look better, no doubt about it.

LYUBOV ANDREYEVNA: Yes. My nerves are better, that's true. (*She is handed her hat and coat.*) I sleep well. Bring me my things, Yasha. It's time. (*To Anya.*) My little girl, we'll see each other again soon . . . I'll go to Paris, live there on the money which your great aunt from Yaroslavl sent to buy the estate. Long live your great aunt! But that money won't last long.

ANYA: Mama, you'll come back soon, soon . . . Isn't that true? I'll study and pass the high-school examination, and then I'll work and help you. Mama, we'll read all kinds of books together. Isn't that true? (*Kisses her mother's hands.*) We'll read on autumn evenings, we'll read a lot of books, and a new, miraculous world will open up before us . . . (*Daydreams.*) Mama, you'll come back . . .

LYUBOV ANDREYEVNA: I'll come back, my precious. (*Hugs her daughter.*)

Lopakhin enters. Charlotta quietly sings a little song.

GAYEV: Happy Charlotta, she's singing!

CHARLOTTA: (*Picks up a bundle and holds it to look like a baby wrapped in a blanket.*) My little baby, lullaby, lullaby . . . (*The baby's crying is heard: "Wa! Wa! . . ."*) Quiet, my pretty one, my dear little boy. ("*Wa! . . . Wa! . . .*") I'm so sorry for you! (*She throws the bundle down.*) Please, find me a position. I can't stand it like this.

LOPAKHIN: We'll find something, Charlotta Ivanovna, don't worry.

GAYEV: They're all leaving us, Varya's going away . . . We're suddenly unnecessary.

CHARLOTTA: There's nowhere for me to live in town. I have to go away. (*Hums.*) It's all the same . . .

Enter Pishchik.

LOPAKHIN: The miracle of nature!

PISHCHIK: Oh, let me catch my breath . . . I'm tormented . . . My most respected friends . . . Give me some water . . .

GAYEV: Come for money, no doubt. Your humble servant, but I flee temptation[44] . . . (*Exits.*)

PISHCHIK: I haven't been to see you in a long time . . . My beauteous lady . . . (*To Lopakhin.*) You're here too . . . Glad to see you . . . A person with a huge mind . . . Take this . . . Here you are . . . (*Hands Lopakhin some money.*) Four hundred rubles . . . That leaves eight hundred forty that I still owe . . .

LOPAKHIN: (*Shrugs his shoulders in bewilderment.*) It's like a dream . . . Where did you get this?

PISHCHIK: Wait a minute . . . It's hot in here . . . The most unusual occurrence. Some Englishmen came to see me and found some kind of white clay on my land[45] . . . (*To Lyubov Andreyevna.*) And for you four hundred . . . You beautiful, amazing woman . . . (*Hands her money.*) The rest later. (*Drinks some water.*) Just now a certain young man in the train told me that a certain . . . a great philosopher advises you to jump off

---

44. A common saying when avoiding something unpleasant.

45. Soil rich in clay is difficult to cultivate, but can be mined for any number of manufacturing uses. The clay may also suggest the presence of oil.

the roof . . . "Jump!" he says, and that will solve everything. (*Surprised.*) Imagine that! Water! . . .

LOPAKHIN: Who are these Englishmen?

PISHCHIK: I leased them a piece of the land with the clay on it for twenty-four years. And now, excuse me, I have no time . . . I'll tell you later . . . I'm going to Znóikov . . . and to Kardamónov[46] . . . I owe everybody . . . (*Drinks.*) I just wanted to say hello . . . Thursday, I'll drop by . . .

LYUBOV ANDREYEVNA: We're leaving for town now, and tomorrow I'll be abroad . . .

PISHCHIK: What? (*Alarmed.*) Why to town? So that's why I see the furniture . . . suitcases . . . Well, it's nothing . . . (*Through tears.*) Nothing . . . People of great minds . . . these English . . . Nothing . . . Be happy . . . God will help you . . . Nothing . . . Everything on this earth comes to an end . . . (*Kisses Lyubov Andreyevna's hand.*) And if you hear rumor that my end has come, remember that . . . that very same horse, and say, "There was on earth a certain so and so . . . a Simeonov-Pishchik . . . May he rest in peace" . . . Wonderful weather . . . Yes . . . (*Exits greatly disconcerted, but immediately returns and says at the door.*) Dashenka sends her regards! (*Exits.*)

LYUBOV ANDREYEVNA: Now we can go. I'm leaving with two worries. The first—Firs is sick. (*Looking at her watch.*) We still have five minutes.

ANYA: Mama, they already took Firs to the hospital. Yasha sent him this morning.

LYUBOV ANDREYEVNA: My second worry is Varya. She's used to getting up early and working, and now without her work she's like a fish out of water. She's getting thin, getting pale, and she cries, poor thing . . . (*Pause.*) You know very well, Yermolay Alekseyevich, that I've dreamed . . . of giving you Varya's hand, and it seemed obvious to everyone that you would marry her. (*Whispers to Anya, then nods to Charlotta; both exit.*) She loves you, you're fond of her, and I don't know, I don't know why you avoid each other. I don't understand!

LOPAKHIN: I have to admit I don't understand it either. It's all so strange somehow . . . If there's still some time, I'm ready right

46. These two names mean "heat wave" and "cardamom."

now . . . Let's finish this off immediately, and be done with it. But without you I feel that I won't propose.

LYUBOV ANDREYEVNA: Excellent. After all, you only need a minute. I'll call her right now . . .

LOPAKHIN: There's champagne at the ready, too! (*Looking at the glasses.*) They're empty, someone's drunk it all. (*Yasha hiccups.*) That's what you'd call really lapping it up . . .

LYUBOV ANDREYEVNA: (*In a lively manner.*) Wonderful. We'll leave you . . . Yasha, *allez!*[47] I'll call her . . . (*At the door.*) Varya, drop everything and come here. Come on! (*Exits with Yasha.*)

LOPAKHIN: (*Looking at his watch.*) Yes . . . (*Pause.*)

Behind the door, a stifled laugh, whispers, finally Varya enters.

VARYA: (*Examines the baggage for a long time.*) It's strange, I can't seem to find . . .

LOPAKHIN: What are you looking for?

VARYA: I packed it myself and I can't remember where.

Pause.

LOPAKHIN: Where are you going now, Varvara Mikhailovna?

VARYA: Me? To the Ragúlins . . . I agreed to look after the household for them . . . A housekeeper, I guess you'd say.

LOPAKHIN: Is that in Yáshnevo? That's about forty-three miles. (*Pause.*) So life in this house is finished . . .

VARYA: (*Examining the baggage.*) Where can it be . . . Maybe I put it in the trunk . . . Yes, life in this house is finished . . . There won't be anymore . . .

LOPAKHIN: I'm going to Kharkov right now . . . on the same train. A lot of business there. I'm leaving Yepikhodov here on the property . . . I've hired him.

VARYA: Well!

47. "Go!" (French).

LOPAKHIN: Last year at this time it had already snowed, if you remember, and now it's quiet, sunny. Only it's cold . . . Three degrees below freezing.

VARYA: I didn't look. (*Pause.*) Besides, our thermometer is broken.

> *Pause. A voice at the door from outside:*
> *"Yermolay Alekseyevich! . . ."*

LOPAKHIN: (*As if he had been waiting for this call.*) Right away! (*Exits quickly.*)

> *Varya sits on the floor, puts her head on a bundle*
> *tied up with a scarf, and quietly sobs, The door*
> *opens, Lyubov Andreyevna enters cautiously.*

LYUBOV ANDREYEVNA: Well? (*Pause.*) We must go.

VARYA: (*No longer crying, wipes her eyes.*) Yes, it's time, Mamochka. I'll make it to the Ragulins today, if I don't miss the train . . .

LYUBOV ANDREYEVNA: (*At the door.*) Anya, put on your coat!

> *Anya enters, then Gayev, Charlotta Ivanovna; Gayev*
> *wears a warm cloth coat with a hood. Servants and*
> *coachmen come in. Yepikhodov fusses near the baggage.*

LYUBOV ANDREYEVNA: Now we can be on our way.

ANYA: (*Joyfully.*) On our way!

GAYEV: My friends, my dears, my darling ones! In forsaking this house forever, how can I keep quiet, how can I refrain from expressing at parting, those feelings which now fill my whole being . . .

ANYA: (*Pleadingly.*) Uncle!

VARYA: Uncle dear, it's not necessary!

GAYEV: (*Despondently.*) Yellow ball, rebound to the center . . . I'll keep quiet . . .

> *Enter Trofimov, then Lopakhin.*

TROFIMOV: Well, ladies and gentlemen, time to leave!

LOPAKHIN: Yepikhodov, my coat!

LYUBOV ANDREYEVNA: I'll sit down for one minute.[48] I feel as if I've never seen what the walls of this house are like, what the ceilings are like, and now I look at them with such a thirst, with such tender love . . .

GAYEV: I remember when I was six years old, on Trinity Sunday,[49] I sat at this window and watched my father walk to church . . .

LYUBOV ANDREYEVNA: Are the things ready?

LOPAKHIN: It seems so. Everything's set. (*To Yepikhodov, putting on his coat.*) Make sure, Yepikhodov, that you keep everything in order.

YEPIKHODOV: (*Talks in a hoarse voice.*) Rest easy, Yermolay Alekseyevich!

LOPAKHIN: What's wrong with your voice?

YEPIKHODOV: I just drank some water and swallowed something.

YASHA: (*With contempt.*) Ignoramus . . .

LYUBOV ANDREYEVNA: We'll go and not a soul will be here . . .

LOPAKHIN: Not until spring.

VARYA: (*Pulling an umbrella out of a bundle in a way that looks as if she were going to hit someone; Lopakhin pretends that he is afraid.*) What are you . . . What . . . I didn't mean to . . .

TROFIMOV: Ladies and gentlemen, let's go to the carriages . . . It's time! The train's coming soon!

VARYA: Petya, here they are, your galoshes, near this suitcase. (*With tears in her eyes.*) How dirty they are, how old . . .

TROFIMOV: (*Putting on the galoshes.*) Let's go, ladies and gentlemen!

---

48. Before leaving for a journey, Russians customarily sit for a few moments. This custom invokes good luck for the trip and for a safe return.

49. In the Christian calendar, this day falls one week after Pentecost, when the Holy Spirit visited Christ's apostles as a tongue of flame. Pentecost is fifty days after Easter.

GAYEV: (*Greatly embarrassed, afraid of crying.*) The train . . . The station . . . A spot to the center, the cue ball rebounds to the corner . . .

LYUBOV ANDREYEVNA: Let's go!

LOPAKHIN: Everyone's here? No one's left in there? (*Locks the side door on the left.*) The things are staying in here so we have to lock up. Let's go! . . .

ANYA: Goodbye, house! Goodbye, old life!

TROFIMOV: Hello, new life! . . . (*Exits with Anya.*)

*Varya glances at the room and exits without hurrying.
Yasha and Charlotta with her dog exit.*

LOPAKHIN: So then, until spring. Let's go out this way, ladies and gentlemen . . . Until next time! . . . (*Exits.*)

Lyubov Andreyevna and Gayev remain together. They seem to have been waiting for this, and throw their arms around each other, but hold back their sobs, crying quietly, afraid to be heard.

GAYEV: (*In despair.*) My sister, my sister . . .

LYUBOV ANDREYEVNA: Oh, my sweet, my tender, my beautiful orchard! . . . My life, my youth, my happiness, goodbye! . . . Goodbye! . . .

Voice of Anya, happily calling: "Mama! . . ."

Voice of Trofimov, happily, excitedly: "Yoo-hoo! . . ."

LYUBOV ANDREYEVNA: The last time I'll look at the walls, the windows . . . Our late mother loved to walk around this room . . .

GAYEV: My sister, my sister! . . .

Voice of Anya: "Mama! . . ."

Voice of Trofimov: "Yoo-hoo! . . ."

LYUBOV ANDREYEVNA: We're coming! . . . (*They exit.*)

The stage is empty. A key is heard locking the door, then the carriages
are heard leaving. It becomes quiet. In the silence the dull sound of the
axe cutting the trees is heard, sounding lonely and sad. Footsteps are
heard; Firs appears at the door to the right. He is dressed, as always, in a
jacket and a white waistcoat. On his feet he wears slippers. He is sick.

FIRS: (*Approaches the door, tries the doorknob.*) Locked. They
     left . . . (*Sits on the divan.*) Forgot about me . . . It's nothing . . .
     I'll sit here a while . . . I'll bet Leonid Andreyevich didn't put
     on the fur coat, but went out in the cloth coat . . . (*Sighs wor-
     riedly.*) And I didn't see to it. Young and green! (*Mumbles
     something that cannot be understood.*) Life has passed by as
     if it were never lived . . . (*Lies down.*) I'll lie down a while . . .
     You don't have your strength now, do you? Nothing's left,
     nothing . . . Ah you . . . Nincompoop! . . . (*Lies still.*)

A distant sound is heard, as if coming from the sky—the sound of a
snapping string, dying away, sad. The silence descends and only the
faraway sound of the axe chopping the trees in the orchard is heard.

Curtain.

A Selected Bibliography in English

Biographies of Anton Chekhov

Callow, Phillip. *Chekhov, The Hidden Ground: A Biography.* Chicago: Ivan R. Dee, 1998.

McVay, Gordon. *Chekhov: A Life in Letters.* London: Folio Society, 1994.

Rayfield, Donald. *Anton Chekhov: A Life.* New York: Henry Holt, 1997.

Simmons, Ernest J. *Chekhov: A Biography.* Chicago: The University of Chicago Press, 1962.

Collections of Chekhov's Stories, Letters, and the Complete Plays

Benedetti, Jean, trans. and ed. *The Moscow Art Theatre Letters.* New York: Routledge, 1991. [Includes letters by and to Chekhov, Knipper, Nemirovich-Danchenko, Stanislavsky, and other members of the Moscow Art Theatre.]

———, trans. and ed. *Dear Writer, Dear Actress: The Love Letters of Anton Chekhov and Olga Knipper.* Hopewell, NJ: Ecco Press, 1997.

Chekhov, Anton. *The Selected Letters of Anton Chekhov.* New York: Farrar, Straus, 1955.

———. *The Undiscovered Chekhov: Forty-Three New Stories.* Translated by Peter Constantine. New York: Seven Stories Press, 1998. [Includes very early stories, usually excluded from anthologies.]

———. *Stories.* Translated by Richard Pevear and Larissa Volokhonsky. New York: Bantam Books, 2000.

———. *The Complete Plays.* Translated and edited by Laurence Senelick. New York: W. W. Norton, 2006. [Includes all of Chekhov's plays and their multiple revisions.]

Garnett, Constance, trans. and ed. *Letters of Anton Chekhov to Olga Knipper.* New York: Blom, 1968.

Karlinsky, Simon, and Michael Henry Heim, trans. and eds. *Anton Chekhov's Life and Thought: Selected Letters.* Berkeley: University of California at Berkeley Press, 1975.

Critical Studies on Chekhov's Dramaturgy

Adler, Stella. *Stella Adler on Ibsen, Strindberg, and Chekhov.* Edited by Barry Paris. New York: Alfred A. Knopf, 1999.

Allen, David. *Performing Chekhov.* New York: Routledge, 2000.

Barricelli, Jean-Pierre, ed. *Chekhov's Great Plays: A Critical Anthology.* New York: New York University Press, 1981. [Includes essays by major scholars.]

Beckerman, Bernard. "Dramatic Analysis and Literary Interpretation: *The Cherry Orchard* as Exemplum." *New Literary History: A Journal of Thought and Interpretation* 2:3 (Spring 1971): 391–406.

———. "The Artifice of 'Reality' in Chekhov and Pinter." *Modern Drama* 21 (1978): 153–61.

Bely, Andrey. "The Cherry Orchard," in Laurence Senelick, trans. and ed., *Russian Dramatic Theory from Puskin to the Symbolists.* Austin: University of Texas Press, 1981.

Bentley, Eric. "Craftsmanship in *Uncle Vanya*," in *In Search of Theatre.* London: Dennis Dobson, 1954.

Blair, Rhonda. "Translation, Image, Action and Chekhov's *The Seagull*," in *The Actor, Image and Action: Acting and Cognitive Neuroscience.* New York: Rouledge, 2008.

Bloom, Harold, ed. *Anton Chekhov: Bloom's Major Dramatists.* Bromall, PA: Chelsea House, 2000. [This anthology includes biographical information, plot summaries of the plays, and critical essays by various authors.]

Brustein, Robert. "Anton Chekhov," in *The Theatre of Revolt.* Boston: Little, Brown, 1964.

Carnicke, Sharon Marie. "Stanislavsky's Production of *The Cherry Orchard* in the U.S." in J. Douglas Clayton, ed., *Chekhov Then and Now: The Reception of Chekhov in World Culture.* New York: Peter Lang, 1997. [An anthology of interesting essays.]

———. "Translating Chekhov's Plays without Russian, or The Nasty Habit of Adaptation" in Michael C. Finke and Julie de Sherbinin, eds., *Chekhov the Immigrant: Translating a Cultural Icon.* Bloomington, IN: Slavica, 2007. [A collection of articles.]

Crittendon, Cole M., "Playing with Time: Chekhov's Drama and Modernism." *The Bulletin of the North American Chekhov Society* 17:1 (Winter 2010): 1–18.

Clyman, Toby W., ed. *A Chekhov Companion.* Westport, CT: Greenwood Press, 1985. [A collection of articles by major scholars.]

De Maegd-Soëp, Carolina. *Chekhov and Women: Women in the Life and Work of Chekhov.* Bloomington, IN: Slavica, 1987.

Emeljanow, Victor, ed. *Chekhov: The Critical Heritage*. Boston: Routledge and Kegan Paul, 1981.

Finke, Michael C. *Seeing Chekhov: Life and Art*. Ithaca: Cornell University Press, 2005.

Gilman, Richard. *Chekhov's Plays: An Opening into Eternity*. New Haven: Yale University Press, 1995.

Gottlieb, Vera. *Chekhov and the Vaudeville: A Study of Chekhov's One Act Plays*. New York: Cambridge University Press, 1982.

———, trans. and ed. *Anton Chekhov at the Moscow Art Theatre: Illustrations of the Original Productions*. New York: Routledge, 2005. [A book of wonderful photographs.]

Gottlieb, Vera, and Paul Allain, eds. *The Cambridge Companion to Chekhov*. Cambridge: Cambridge University Press, 2000. [An anthology of critical articles.]

Jackson, Robert Louis, ed. *Chekhov: A Collection of Critical Essays*. Englewood Cliffs, NJ: Prentice-Hall, 1967. [Includes essays by major scholars from Russia.]

Koteliansky, S. S., ed. *Anton Tchekhov* [sic]: *Literary and Theatrical Reminiscences*. New York: Haskell House, 1974.

Levin, Irina, and Igor Levin. *Working on the Play and the Role: The Stanislavsky Method for Analyzing the Characters in a Drama*. Chicago: Ivan R. Dee, 1992. [Uses *The Cherry Orchard* to describe acting technique.]

Loehlin, James, N. *Chekhov: The Cherry Orchard*. Cambridge: Cambridge University Press, 2006.

Magarshack, David. *Chekhov as a Dramatist*. New York: Hill and Wang, 1968.

McVay, Gordon. *Chekhov's* Three Sisters. London: Bristol Classical Press, 1995.

Nemirovitch-Dantchenko [sic], Vladimir. *My Life in the Russian Theatre*. Boston: Little, Brown, 1937.

Peace, Richard. *Chekhov: A Study of the Four Major Plays*. New Haven: Yale University Press, 1983.

Pervukhina, Natalia. *Anton Chekhov: The Sense and the Nonsense*. New York: Legas, 1993. [An excellent study of Chekhov's use of humor and absurdity.]

Pitcher, Harvey J. *The Chekhov Play: A New Interpretation*. New York: Barnes and Noble, 1973.

———. *Chekhov's Leading Lady: A Portrait of the Actress Olga Knipper*. New York: F. Watts, 1980.

Rayfield, Donald. *Chekhov's* Uncle Vania *and* The Wood Demon. London: Bristol Classical Press, 1995.

————. *The Cherry Orchard: Catastrophe and Comedy.* New York: Twayne Publishers, 1994.

————. *Understanding Chekhov: A Critical Study of Chekhov's Prose and Drama.* Madison: University of Wisconsin Press, 1999.

Reid, John McKellor. *The Polemical Force of Chekhovian Comedies: A Rhetorical Analysis.* Lewiston, NY: Edwin Mellen Press, 2007.

Senelick, Laurence. *Anton Chekhov.* New York: Grove Press, 1985.

————. *The Chekhov Theatre: A Century of the Plays in Performance.* New York: Cambridge University Press, 1997.

Stanislavski [sic], K. S. *My Life in Art.* Translated by J. J. Robbins. New York: Theatre Arts Books, 1948. [This is the classic translation.]

————. *My Life in Art.* Translated by Jean Benedetti. New York: Routledge, 2008.

Stelleman, Jenny. *Aspects of Dramatic Communication: Action, Non-Action, Interaction.* Amsterdam: Rodopi, 1992. [Includes discussion of Chekhov and two other Russian dramatists: the symbolist A. Blok and the absurdist D. Kharms.]

Styan, J. L. *Chekhov in Performance: A Commentary on the Major Plays.* New York: Cambridge University Press, 1971.

Tait, Peta. *Performing Emotions: Gender, Bodies, Spaces, in Chekhov's Drama and Stanislavski's Theatre.* Aldershot, UK: Ashgate, 2003.

Tulloch, John. *Chekhov: A Structuralist Study.* Totowa, NJ: Barnes and Noble, 1980.

Valency, Maurice. *The Breaking Sting: The Plays of Anton Chekhov.* New York: Schocken Books, 1983. [A classic study of Chekhov's drama.]

Wellek, René, and Nonna D. Wellek, eds. *Chekhov: New Perspectives.* Englewood Cliffs, NJ: Prentice-Hall, 1984. [An anthology of major critical essays.]

Worall, Nick, ed. *File on Chekhov.* New York: Methuen, 1986. [A concise and useful chronology of information.]